The End of Advertising

The End of Advertising

Why It Had to Die, and the Creative Resurrection to Come

Andrew Essex

Spiegel & Grau
New York

Published in the United States by Spiegel & Grau,
an imprint of Random House, a division of
Penguin Random House LLC, New York.

SPIEGEL & GRAU and Design is a registered trademark of
Penguin Random House LLC.

Library of Congress Cataloging-in-Publication Data
Names: Essex, Andrew, author.
Title: The end of advertising : why it had to die, and
the creative resurrection to come / Andrew Essex.
Description: New York : Spiegel & Grau, 2017.
Identifiers: LCCN 2016049623 | ISBN 9780399588518 (hardback) |
ISBN 9780399588525 (ebook)
Subjects: LCSH: Advertising. | Advertising—Audio-visual
equipment. | Branding (Marketing) |
BISAC: BUSINESS & ECONOMICS / Advertising & Promotion. |
BUSINESS & ECONOMICS / Marketing / General. |
SOCIAL SCIENCE / Popular Culture.
Classification: LCC HF5823 .E88 2017 | DDC 659.1—dc23
LC record available at https://lccn.loc.gov/2016049623

Printed in the United States of America on acid-free paper

randomhousebooks.com
spiegelandgrau.com

2 4 6 8 9 7 5 3 1

First Edition

To my family,
for never blocking me,
even when I'm annoying

Who has empowered you to peddle round your indulgences from divine ordinations? The hairs on our head are numbered, and the days of our lives. False negotiator, away!

—"The Lightning-Rod Man,"
Herman Melville, 1854

Advertising's worth to civilization depends on how it is being used.

—from a J. Walter Thompson
new business presentation, circa 1925

If your left hand sees how much fun your right hand is having, it won't want to be left out.

—Advertising Hall of Fame inductee
Bill Cosby, for Jell-O Gelatin Pops, 1982

Contents

Part One

Adblockalypse Now

The Beginning of the End

I t was the summer of 2015 and Howard Stern was hysterical.

That the legendary shock jock could be so easily enraged was certainly nothing new. In this instance, however, it was the *subject* of Stern's apoplectic ire that was truly exceptional: The King of All Media was ranting about *advertising,* and how much he *despised* it.

Stern was throwing a hissy fit because he'd just heard about an inspired technology called AdBlock Plus, an ingenious app specifically conceived, as its not especially inspired name suggested, to block ads, to eradicate them like bison from the prairie, to disappear them once and for all from your online ecosystem.

By simply downloading the AdBlock extension to Chrome, Safari, or any other popular browser, one could be forever liberated from such noxious pollutants as "pre-roll" and "banners," those (mostly) annoying promotional videos and (almost always) irksome boxes that contaminate most people's Web experience.

"I fucking *hate* ads on the Internet," Stern raged. He's a man who expects to be on top of technology, and who pays others well for the privilege. Having discovered that AdBlock had in fact been around for years (as had several rivals, not to mention a host of platforms conceived to bypass ads that date back to TiVo), he was reaming his IT team with the wrath of a thirsty man who'd just lost his directions to the oasis. "I'm sitting through these ads and *you're telling me there's a way to AVOID them?!*"

That Stern's radio show is in fact lousy with ads created a certain eyebrow-raising dissonance, but I suspect few listeners disagreed with the sentiment. After all, people may love brands, but *nobody actually likes advertising* (except on Super Bowl Sunday, the high holiday of my former industry).

But ads were just a fact of life, right, like the common cold? Insufferable and incurable and as entrenched in our media picnic basket as apple pie. Long before the Internet, when "appointment" TV ruled the land, commercials—minus about fifty iconic exceptions from 1948 to 1984—had long been a form of *capitulation,* a necessary evil endured by consumers in exchange for the free content they'd actually come to see. Most of us understood on some level that this was how the rent was paid, but no one was especially happy about it.

Stern surely intuited that shitting on advertising was pure populist red meat, something everybody could agree on, a gift-wrapped insight he could milk for twenty minutes of airtime, or until the next Squatty Potty spot.

Our story might end there, a momentary wormhole in the church-and-state wall between media and marketing, were it not for the fact that Stern wasn't the only ad-supported executive expressing irony-free disdain for commercial interruption that strange summer. If he had considered events from earlier that June, Stern would've found himself in common cause with an unlikely bedfellow: Larry Page, CEO and cofounder of Google, aka Alphabet.

At Google's 2015 annual shareholder meeting, Page reportedly told marketers that they needed to "get better at producing ads *that are less annoying*" (italics mine), and that he had no intention of interfering with the rise of ad-blocking technology on Google's ubiquitous Chrome browser. Which was odd, given that YouTube, a Google subsidiary, had cleared $1.13 billion in ad revenue in 2014, according to *The Wall Street Journal,* a windfall generated by the very same ads that Larry Page, Howard Stern—and, let's be honest, pretty much anyone with a pulse—didn't like very much.

Odder still was that the dream of a world filled with

less annoying ads had been around for a very, very long time—decades, actually—albeit elusively. A 1969 survey determined that 51 percent of all young people between the ages of fourteen and twenty-five found television advertising—wait for it—*annoying*. It should be mentioned that the Magazine Publishers of America, who claimed, conveniently, that only 13 percent of the population were annoyed by magazine ads, conducted this '69 survey.

At any rate, here in the twenty-first century, where one had to search long and hard for a single fourteen-to-twenty-five-year-old who'd ever watched appointment TV or read a magazine, Google clearly appeared conflicted. Yes, the company had profited handsomely from Internet advertising, but boy, was that advertising annoying. Yes, people needed to sell things; serving ads to large audiences was historically how marketers moved the merch. Search, where Google made its big money, was one thing, and who could truly dislike the pure utility of search? (Even though search results are often paid, i.e., advertising.)

But those hateful pre-roll ads on YouTube (which were more annoying, and also less profitable to Google, than its search revenue), and those dreaded banner ads that stalked one around the Internet like an obsessed former lover in need of a restraining order? Oy, well, now *those* were clearly doing harm (a violation of the company's infamous "Don't be evil" edict), the proof being that millions of people and one celebrity DJ were stampeding to download software deliberately conceived to escape them.

So why am I telling you all this? What's eating your irritable author? Good questions.

The fact is, I'm a former ad guy myself, a retired shark in a gray flannel suit. I logged a decade of service at one of the finest advertising firms in the world, if not the finest, first as CEO, then as vice chairman. If a *Mad Men* reference can put things in perspective, I played the Roger Sterling role. My former firm made—and continues to make—the best ads in the business, dominating the industry with exponential growth and cleaning up at myriad award shows.

But for most of my time in the ad game, I was conflicted. Yes, I worked at the best shop, one that produced inspired work, but we were the exception to the rule. The worst elements of the industry, which is to say most of it, didn't make much that was particularly good for the planet. None were doing any evil, but—with several exceptions (pro bono work, internships, presidential campaigns)—most traditional advertising wasn't adding value to society. Mainly, average advertising just helped sell stuff. Please don't mistake me for a Bernie Sanders–

style socialist raging against the evils of capitalism. I *love* capitalism. I love the marketplace. I love products. I'm soothed by retail therapy. I'm jelly in the hands of the compelling power of a well-pitched brand.

But here's the odd part: My dislike for the worst elements of the business made me an ad guy who increasingly hated advertising, which made it tricky to do my job.

Part of the problem was the constant grind of toiling in an industry almost exclusively known for peddling, the curse of being secondary rather than primary, of being associated with the smirking interloper at the party who brought the beer rather than the glamorous and gracious host.

Another pain point was traditional advertising's unfortunate tradition of inauthenticity and hucksterism, of knowing that the increasingly haggard face I woke up to every morning could sell ice to Eskimos with effortless ease. Perhaps I should have run for president.

An ever expanding sense of self-loathing weighed heavily on my heart, dear reader, though the fact that I was paid well certainly eased the pain. Then again, there's really no amount of cash, unless you're a total mercenary, that can erase the sting of having to proudly shill "liquefied cow parts," as a former colleague at a lesser agency called his client's top-selling sandwich.

But as they say during game shows to goose the audience: *And that's not all.*

Because here's my other not-so-dark secret, and why I bring a unique perspective to the table: I wasn't always an ad man. Long before I infiltrated Madison Avenue, I spent two decades in publishing. I was an editor and writer at some of the best magazines on earth, including *The New Yorker* and others. I also launched fluff like *Us Weekly* and covered the Hollywood-industrial complex for *Details* and *Entertainment Weekly,* among others.

For a long time, working in the magazine business felt much as it must have felt to work in the music business during its heyday. The gig was glamorous; we swaggered with the illuminati clout of those who decide what matters.

The problem was that despite all that swagger, I had no idea how the magazines I worked for made money. I knew it came from ad and subscription revenue, of course, but the details and the selling thereof were somebody else's problem. The magazine business, like the newspaper business, was set up as a tale of two teams: church and state.

I was one of the high priests. My flock put together the magazine. We created the content, which meant we got to steer clear of such vulgar matters as monetization. There was an entirely different staff to deal with the grody business of getting our product paid for. The problem with this model, which still remains in effect in many places today—and which was set up in part to ensure editorial independence—is that it reinforces the reductive cliché that business people can't be creative, and that creative people don't need to handle their own business. It's an undergraduate approach.

Anyway, back at the magazine, this duality was palpably reflected in the final product. There was the content that my colleagues and I put together, the stuff our subscribers paid to see. And then there were the ads, those secondary snacks that somebody else had inserted willy-nilly into our pages, like gate-crashers at a sold-out show.

Now, we priests weren't naive enough to think the ads didn't need to be there. We knew they kept us in expense account clover; sometimes we even went on sales calls to help seduce (or placate) an advertiser. But we totally condescended to the ads. They were not the *real* content. They weren't the thing; they were the thing that sold the thing. We were authentic; ads were all artifice. Unfortunately, what we failed to realize is that content and context are inseparable. When you control only part of the content, you don't control the context.

But then the Internet and social media changed everything. Traditional magazines and newspapers bore the brunt of it, often quite badly. One of the reasons they suffered is that the advertisers woke up and realized, thanks to the many new channels available to audiences, that they could bypass magazines and commune directly with consumers. They didn't have to crash someone else's party, they could experiment more and even create their own main events. The money they were spending on "traditional" print ads was suddenly diverted somewhere "digital."

As magazine publishing contracted, so did the jobs and salaries—which were never very high in the first place, a point that seemed to call into question just how smart those priests were (or perhaps they'd unwittingly taken a vow of poverty). And as with so many other traditional businesses, from the record industry to the Pony Express, the jig was up.

Anyone awake should have seen it coming, or at least in retrospect it clearly appeared obvious. Many in the magazine game realized that the content they'd been creating wasn't all that essential in the first place, and that perhaps they'd been kept afloat by a wobbly ad revenue bubble that had finally burst. Many publications shut down. It turned out the world had more than enough content without them.

My personal Guernica came when the luxury magazine I'd been running folded. I think the owner lost it in a high-stakes poker game in Marbella. I happened to be on a junket in Dubai when I got the news. *C'est la vie.*

I could have found another job in magazines, but it all felt far too familiar, the same old, same old, only older and increasingly irrelevant. I had lost interest in my beloved industry, and I wasn't alone. Magazines, at least in their traditional form, no longer seemed to be where the action was.

It was time to go across the aisle.

When I left to join a fledgling advertising firm, I jokingly told my friends in magazines that I'd "gone to the dark side." That was how they saw it, so it was best to self-deprecate. But I never thought of the move that way for a moment. I was excited. I saw it as moving toward the light. The dark side was what I was leaving behind. Advertising was ripe for massive disruption, and that change could be qualitative. Magazines, meanwhile, had lost their luminescence.

Ten years later, I was presiding over the hottest creative ad firm in the industry, and we'd gotten there by making ads that didn't suck.

The story could easily end there. But something was vexing me besides all the soul-squeezing issues I laid out before. What really worried me was this: I was experiencing a painful feeling of déjà vu. I realized the same thing that had happened to the magazine business was now happening to advertising. It was getting elbowed out. The industry was focusing myopically on content, and all around us the context was crumbling.

What was truly painful was the dawning realization, just as I'd seen with magazines, that traditional advertising was slowly but surely becoming obsolete. It was increasingly clear that advertising, at least as we'd come to know it, was inexorably headed down the path of the blacksmith and typewriter businesses.

Don't get me wrong: The need to sell things will never die. And there were people who had real talent for the selling. But lack of talent wasn't the problem. Firms like mine were often doing incredible and inspired work. The problem was that there were fewer and fewer places where an ad could actually *live*. The very canvas on which Adland painted was receding like a glacier facing global warming.

It's one thing to have doubts about the value of what you do. It's an entirely different matter to see what you do for a living becoming obsolete in real time. Especially if you've seen that same movie before.

And it's particularly weird when you're participating in your own demise.

Block Around the Clock

Here's the thing: It turns out I was just like Howard Stern. Until I happened upon that bit in which Stern praised ad blocking, *I had no idea that such technology ex-*

isted, I'm embarrassed to admit. And I was a leader in the ad business! I was supposed to see the future.

Sure, I knew about TiVo, DVRs, and other time-shifting tech. Like almost everyone else, I'd taken to bingeing on television via ad-free platforms such as Net-flix and iTunes and Amazon Prime. I almost never saw an actual commercial unless I was watching sports or sweating on a treadmill. But I certainly didn't know about blocking.

So, like Stern, I started downloading ad-blocking software. I put it on my laptop and my phone. I did this with the perverse awareness of a professional who knows he's violating a sacred oath. I was subverting the rules of my trade, like a doctor doing harm or a hooker giving a freebie. I watched the software install itself with a sense of wonder. Where would the unwanted ads go? What would take their place? Did it make a satisfying sound like those purple zappers that electrocute insects?

Then I restarted my computer, switched on my phone, and—*voilà*—it was over.

The adpocalypse had begun. And my future, not to mention the future of my $965 billion industry—a global spend *AdAge* says will soon likely exceed $1 trillion—would never be the same.

Bottom line: Life is better without bad ads. It's simply irrefutable. And no matter where you sit in this system, history tells us—or at least our moral expectation of his-

tory tells us—that plague and blight are eventually overcome; peace triumphs over war; love conquers hate;
poverty, disease, and ignorance are eventually vanquished.
The arc of the moral universe is long, but it bends toward justice.
Bad ads, once a scourge like polio or syphilis, were finally facing a remedy. And the solution was free and
easily accessible to consumers. The first shot in the revolution had been fired; Howard and I were only now
hearing the sound.

There would be no turning back. The genie was out
of the bottle.

You know you're looking at a seriously dire situation
when it's okay to mix metaphors.

So I got out.

Okay, I get it. You're a skeptic. Is the traditional ad as we
know it really dead? If so, then why do I keep seeing
them during sporting events? you say. We'll get to that,
but let's look at some of the forces behind the kudzu-like
spread of ad blocking and its dire repercussions.

By the summer of 2015, around the time that Stern
and I got the memo, the rapid growth of ad-blocking
software had become such an acute source of industry
anxiety that media sites like *CBS.com* and *Forbes.com,*
among many others, had resorted to *blocking* ad-blocking
technology, basically extorting viewers to get with the

program. Many encouraged users to "white-list" their sites, i.e., undo those pesky blockers just for them.

One company, Sourcepoint, started by a former Google exec, raised $10 million in venture capital to *block* blocking. Messages such as THIS VIDEO IS UNAVAILABLE BECAUSE WE WERE UNABLE TO LOAD A MESSAGE FROM OUR SPONSOR suggested that the only solution for content interruptus was disabling that nasty ad-blocking software.

The Washington Post started testing ad-blocking blockers on its website. "Without income via advertising, we won't be able to deliver the journalism that people coming to our site expect from us," the *Post* tsk-tsked via official spokesbot.

Yes, strange times were creating strange new allegiances and alliances, new victors and victims, new friends, enemies, and *frenemies,* conflicts and *coopetitions*. It was a brave new world: human sacrifice, dogs and cats living together, mass hysteria, etc.

And things got weirder still. For instance, the ad-blocking companies were *advertising* themselves, which sort of defeated their purpose. Shine, an Israeli ad-blocking player, took out a full-page ad in the *Financial Times* to alert consumers that those especially annoying mobile ads weren't just noise, they were likely gulping down half of your data plan. "Advertisers make billions in mobile advertising," Shine scolded, taking the moral high ground. "Consumers should not have to subsidize their business."

You had to hand it to the publicity-hungry folks at Shine, as well as all the other ambitious insurgents on the ad-blocking scene. *They'd decided to advertise a product that blocked advertising!* That took some balls, or at least a taste for tautology. And in doing so, they were leaning hard into an old argument, the same one that file-sharing renegades such as Napster had effectively leveled against the big bad record companies: *Suck it, old media.* Content wants to be free, get over it. Or rather: Consumers want to be freed from bad content.

And the rewards of ad blocking were certainly compelling. Indeed, why should anyone have to endure anything as annoying as unwanted ads? After all, it was 2015. Power to the people! Maybe some consumers would go so far as to pay a premium to avoid ads. And there was money to be made from this ad-blocking thing: The young guns behind the blocking business realized publishers might pay a vig to have their ads unblocked.

Inside the industry, the summer of '15 debate raged on, fraught with consequence, redolent of massive secular change. Among civilians, it was far more cut and dried. After all, most people don't really care about the economics of the content industrial machine, not to mention the ethical niceties. They just don't want to be annoyed.

What all this hue and cry ultimately meant for the relationship between advertiser and audience, as advertisers behaved more and more like spurned suitors desperate not to be turned away, was anyone's guess. But one could assume it likely wasn't love.

On top of this came more big news that summer: Apple, maker of the competing Safari browser, which permitted ad blocking, was moving to make it easier to block ads on the iPhone, which currently didn't allow ad blocking, by permitting ad blocking on iOS9.

At risk was the fast-growing mobile ad market, which *Business Insider* pegged at $42 billion but *eMarketer* called closer to $100 billion. At stake was the user experience of the mobile-enabled world, which is to say *all of humanity,* most of whom didn't want to be irritated by even more unwelcome, i.e., really small—and thus especially annoying—ads.

How nice that Apple was standing up for the little guy and attempting to keep its iPhone experience uncluttered. It all felt very Jobsian, this interest in a less annoying user experience. That this was a way of firing back at Alphabet (aka Google) was perhaps less obvious. Samsung would later join the scrum, releasing an ad-blocking platform for their Android users and thus getting into a complicated food fight in which the agendas and allegiances, not to mention the outcomes, were opaque at best.

Yes, 2015 was a crazy, worrisome summer for the entire media industry, and as time marched on, the worry only spread wider still. That the likes of Howard Stern, Alphabet, and Apple could so publicly bite the hands that fed them, and that so many industry gatekeepers found their nail-bitten fingers in an increasingly leaky dike, suggested something of an inflection point, an end-times urgency that raised questions about The Future of Advertising. What, exactly, was happening out there?

Then the numbers started coming in, and it turned out that the numbers were shocking, an Antietam for Adland.

According to SourcePoint, one in ten Americans had downloaded ad-blocking software, circa 2015. In Europe, especially in Germany and France, the number was closer to *one in four* people embracing ad blocking. Adobe issued a report that claimed 144 million people were using ad blockers; publishers stood to lose an estimated $21.8 billion in ad revenue. In her 2016 report on Internet trends, the respected industry analyst Mary Meeker would proclaim that some 93 percent of the population had considered using ad-blocking software (while a mere 62 percent were annoyed by ads), and that the global ad-blocking number across mobile and desktop platforms was closer to 420 million.

As the crazy summer of 2015 extended into the even crazier summer of 2016, many of the top apps in the Apple Store remained ad-blocking programs. *Advertising Age* released a humorous cover depicting Times Square devoid of ads—as pure hyperbole, of course. Or was it? *The New York Times* ran a special report to measure how much time ad-blocking software saved you on various platforms, and what the breakdown was between ad data and edit data on mobile news sites (the slowest site was *Boston.com,* which was especially bogged down with sluggish video ads and thus crying out for ad blocking).

The Google Play store was seeing similar trend lines. And what would happen when ad blocking was bundled into ubiquitous antivirus software, predicted to be coming soon to a computer near you?

What did this avalanche of ad blocking portend?

Various ad-supported entities were exploring a variety of responses. Many were publicly concerned. Many more were privately panicking. Others were just pissed off or insouciant. One industry potentate called it "the latest crisis du jour," shrugging off ad blocking as "robbery, plain and simple—an extortionist scheme that exploits consumer disaffection and risks distorting the economics of democratic capitalism."

The implication was that if traditional ads went away, there would simply be no cash left to pay for the content, and the free or highly subsidized services so many of us enjoy would vanish. This was not a victimless crime (not that the *consumers* were criminals or anything; see *The Record Business v. Napster*). None of this response questioned whether regular people cared about the implications, or whether there was any conceivable scenario in which civilians would welcome back those blocked ads once they'd gotten rid of them.

The industry continued to do the math, and the math wasn't pretty. According to some, if consumers truly embraced ad blocking en masse, it would trigger a macro economic collapse, possibly even an outright recession. Absent all that annoying advertising, U.S. consumers would no longer know how to make domestic spending decisions. *OMG, darling, without ads how will I ever know what to buy?* Gagging Madison Avenue would result in a $350 billion loss to America's gross national product, according to the Internet Advertising Bureau.

Publishers, per the IAB, who were already seeing 40 percent of their ad revenue lost to ad blocking, would go out of business. The same report trotted out two Nobel economics laureates to say "Advertising helps the economy function smoothly." It was a wonder the subject wasn't being discussed during the presidential debates.

Advertising, it seemed, was too big to fail.

• • •

Given the stakes, the story needed a villain. So some endeavored to paint ad blocking as a moral hazard. Sure, the software was cool, but this was the tradecraft of unethical *foreign* tech companies "looking to divert ad spending to their own pockets," exploiting our widespread loathing of advertising as a way of realizing their true purpose—a massive shakedown. And there was some truth to this idea that the forces behind the ad-blocking boom were actually the Tony Sopranos of technology. After all, some marketers and publishers were being forced to pay five- or six-figure fees so their beloved ads wouldn't wind up in the seller's equivalent of cement shoes.

It should be noted that ad blocking wasn't the only villain haunting Madison Avenue. Though the blockers were definitely public enemy number one, the industry was also dealing with cord cutters, time-shifting, and perhaps most troubling, the widespread blight of so-called "ad fraud." Ad fraud was when unsavory platforms, publishers, or media buying companies assured an advertiser that their message had appeared, when it might *never* have appeared at all, or it was shown less often than promised, or the number of people who'd actually seen the ad in question had been extremely inflated. That summer of 2015, ad fraud was, and remained, a very big problem. The following year, the ad industry would have another headache thanks to a trade organization's contentious exposé on advertising "rebates," a euphemism for kickbacks, a fairly widespread practice in which the buyers of advertising extort money back from the sellers.

But there was one major difference: Ad fraud and kickbacks were the essence of inside baseball. Joe Consumer didn't care much about fraud or scams being perpetrated on an industry he held in such low esteem. These subjects only mattered to industry people. Ad blocking, on the other hand, mattered to regular people. And regular people mattered.

Meanwhile, many in the industry continued to write off ad blocking as an aberration, the work of a few rotten apples; as with ad fraud, it was much ado about nothing. It would surely fade away. Unfortunately, it wasn't nothing, and there wasn't much anyone could do to stop it.

If you hovered thirty thousand feet up, in search of some perspective, far above the chronic myopia of Madison Avenue, it was clear to anyone with vision that the industry was in serious trouble, far more serious than many realized. And the impending sense of doom felt by many, a nagging sense that the end was nigh, seemed entirely justifiable.

The adblockians were at the gate.

• • •

Let me tell you more about my own first experience with ad blocking, and why my story might just as well be yours.

One night, in the early fall of 2015, I found myself stuck with a device on which I'd failed to download ad-blocking software. Irritated by an ad that kept popping up on my digital version of *The New York Times,* a "paper" that I have long since read exclusively via tablet, I took matters into my own hands.

Let me begin by saying that I love *The New York Times*. I have written for the *Times;* I have consulted for the *Times*. I have dear friends who have toiled at the *Times* for years. They're fine, smart people, committed to a noble, indispensable enterprise that transcends mere commerce. I believe that the health of *The New York Times* is directly connected to the health of society, and that it would be a mortal blow to civilization if the *Times* were to die.

Oh, but this terrible ad. It was an unpleasant excrescence brought to you by a third-tier financial services company. I will do the honorable thing and not identify the company, nor will I expose the people who produced the "creative." But it wasn't just annoying; it was cheesy, overwritten, oversized, tone-deaf, outmoded, wrong in every conceivable way. Moreover, I wasn't interested in the subject matter, and not even remotely persuaded to click on it, let alone look at it for longer than the time it took to look away. *The ad was trying to sell me something I didn't want,* and instead it was making me feel a deep loathing for the seller. It was woefully uncouth in its proximity to news of great consequence and sobriety, not only distracting me from stories about the latest gun massacre, Putin's follies, and ISIS, but sticking out like a sore thumb, a dweeb in a garish sweater standing next to a supermodel. Howard Stern, I feel your pain.

Please know I am not picking on the *Times,* but rather on the antiquated and increasingly incongruent practice of putting an ad next to something else, which is called an adjacency, the thing plopped next to my thing that I ignored when I was a magazine guy.

The irony is that an adjacent ad was the model we'd accepted for years, at least when the newspaper was the reigning medium. We'd accepted that it was standard operating procedure to arbitrarily insert a message *between* the stories we were reading. In 1906, advertising executive James Collins confessed to the U.S. Congress, "There is still an illusion to the effect that a magazine is a periodical in which advertising is incidental. But we don't look at it that way. A magazine is simply a device to induce people to read advertising."

But now, decades later, despite historic innovation, we

were still applying the same construct to an entirely different context, using an outdated metaphor in a far more convoluted era. It was like taking a stagecoach to a Monster Truck freestyle show and expecting it to keep up. We didn't have to accept this adjacency model anymore. It no longer made sense.

Back on my couch, digitally reading the *Times,* I stopped for a moment and downloaded the blocking software. And, boom, there went that ugly ad—there went all the ads—with the ease of a dermatologist's scalpel swiping a mole.

For a moment, I felt a little uncomfortable. As a person who spent his entire professional life at the intersection of media and marketing, I was fully aware what a dire zero-sum game that I, and all the blockers out there, were playing. The implications were devastating, like being given possession of the nuclear football without knowing the code.

In downloading this software and enjoying an ad-free experience, I was garroting my beloved *New York Times* and other media sites. I was strangling their ad revenue, cutting off monetary oxygen and thus commencing the shutdown of the seller's central nervous system. I was actively participating in the demise of an institution I hold dear. I was part of the problem, not the solution. Or was I?

Which raised several interesting questions. Who, exactly, was at fault here? Should a reader still be required to endure something he or she didn't ask to see in order to read/watch what he or she actually came for? In the case of the *Times,* and other premium content providers, I was doing my part by paying for this product via my subscription. I was among those willing to cough up cash for their content, and rightly so. However, I had become unwilling to wade through their spurious ads or even look upon their ugliness; I'd uncovered a superior experience without ads, and, like anyone given a better offer, there was no way I was going back.

Was that my problem or theirs? Was it the reader's concern that the content provider's cost structure required dual revenue streams? Or that one of those streams annoyed the hell out of so many, myself included? And why had no one at the *Times* asked me if I'd consider paying a premium to *never* see ads, rather than allowing me to take matters into my own paws?

Meanwhile, as a result of giving away their content for years, a strategy that seemed like the right thing to do at the time, the *Times* and others of their ilk had inadvertently habituated a new generation of young people, people with much less respect for their legacy, to believe that their premium content was supposed to be free.

Unfortunately, this represented a double whammy, as this much younger generation, kids raised in an unprecedented age of cord cutting and blocking software, had trouble even understanding the rudimentary premise of ads, on the rare occasions they saw them. As with paying for content, the whole idea of unwanted interruption was essentially alien to them; it was inexplicable, actually.

Unlike my generation, weaned on the bargain of being interrupted by something we didn't want in exchange for something we did, these new kids—sometimes erroneously called millennials, but more accurately (if unimaginatively) known as Generation Z—will be the first generation to come of age in a world in which one can consume vast amounts of content, maybe even all of one's content needs (with the exception of live sports), without ever so much as seeing a traditional ad, or seeing ads fairly infrequently.

Maybe we should call them the Blocking Boomers? And would a generation fundamentally unfamiliar with such inconvenience ever ex parte embrace it?

Anyway, don't just take my word for it. I know this with some degree of certainty because I live with one of these kids.

Yes, I have the good fortune of having produced an all-American adolescent boy. By all-American, I mean that my son, like most adolescents, is well versed in the always-on, all-you-can-eat content buffet that is the modern media landscape. He likes to watch boatloads of video, which today mostly means a lot of YouTube, the most popular video service in the world.

It was via YouTube that my son came to know Key & Peele, the brilliant comedy duo, whose program is technically broadcast on Comedy Central, or was until the duo announced their retirement. This distinction is of course meaningless to my son, and to most people born after the year 2000. My kid doesn't connect the content to the channel from which it came. It doesn't really matter to him if a show comes from NBC or HBO or Amazon. It just is, it's always on, and he and his brethren like to consume Key & Peele content over and over, which accounts for the duo's multimillion views.

Unfortunately, as much as my son loved Key & Peele, he *hated* the pre-roll advertising that he was forced to endure every time a skit cued up; it infuriated him, and he did not see any value exchange or understand why he had to watch something he did not ask to see. He found it . . . *rude*. He understood, once I explained, why YouTube would try to monetize their content with advertising, and that it might even get Key & Peele paid. That said, he was not convinced the process worked, and surely wouldn't click on or buy anything from a company that tried to manipulate him in such a ham-fisted fashion.

When I explained the logic, when I explained that

this was just the way it was, and that it had been this way for years, he shrugged and said, "I might be a kid, Dad, but I'm not *stupid*. Is that *really* what they think?" For him, it was a bug, not a feature. (It should be mentioned that as a former ad guy, I enjoyed this what's-up-with-ads conversation far more than our previous conversation about a Viagra commercial, which entailed explaining the downside of a four-hour erection.)

My son might not be stupid, but he had no idea how to solve his pre-roll problem. At first, he was simply stunned. He'd spent his childhood in an ad-free Garden of Eden and suddenly had had his first taste of advertising's befouled fruit. Unlike Howard Stern, he'd failed to get the ad-blocking memo. Not knowing that there was a simple solution out there, he'd resigned himself to actively ignoring all pre-roll until the end of time, and he was *giddy* with excitement when his cutting-edge old man revealed that we could return him to paradise via ad-blocking technology, that his ad-inflicted umbrage could now come to an end. Having heard about this exciting option, he urged me to *immediately* download an ad blocker onto *all* his devices.

The next day, my son and I opened the Apple App Store, typed in "ad blocking," and quickly discovered more than fifty options, ranging from free to $2.99 a pop. Some had generic names; others sported more fanciful, well-branded monikers such as Clear, Crystal,

Ruby, Sumo, and Clean. Others were more transparently prescriptive: Ad Kill, Ad Kill Pro, and my personal favorite, if only for pure allegorical assertiveness, *Freedom*.

I downloaded AdBlock for him and, lo and behold, in less than two minutes, we were reading from several media platforms on my phablet, now blissfully free from ads. Then we watched a bunch of ad-free videos. We were happily saying no to long wait times, and to those infuriating pop-up ads that are Brandland's equivalent of biting flies. My son was finally unshackled from the tedious chains of pre-roll. We were *bonding* over blocking.

"Dad, this is *soooo* much better without the ads," he said.

"You think?" I responded. "But what about the fact that a lot of people won't get paid?"

He shrugged and went back to watching *Key & Peele*. Kids rarely have to consider the consequences of secular change. And there would indeed be consequences. There would be a human cost, and several long-standing livelihoods would never be the same. But even the finest blacksmith had to ultimately admit that a car was something more than a faster horse.

As quaint as it might seem, my little domestic moment nicely captures the massive changes in consumer behavior that the rise of ad blocking has wrought. A few months after our father-son adventure, YouTube announced the arrival of YouTube Red, its entrance into the ad-free subscription model. Now, for a mere ten bucks a month, my son could have all the *Key & Peele* he could handle, minus the annoying pre-roll. No ad blocking required; YouTube just required my credit card in exchange.

"People are embracing paid subscriptions for ad-free content at an incredible pace," said Robert Kyncl, YouTube's Chief Business Officer, to *The New York Times,* stating what was now increasingly obvious. It was as if he'd just spent a week in my home, which, oddly enough, was turning out to be like many homes.

And it wasn't just the execs at YouTube driving this change, it was the talent, too. Take the case of the notorious PewDiePie. In case you're not familiar with the name, i.e., you're *old,* he's the most profitable star on YouTube. In October 2015, Mr. Pie, whose real name is Felix Kjellberg, became a public champion of YouTube Red on Tumblr. Apparently Kjellberg had polled his 6.6 million Twitter followers and discovered that 40 percent of them were using ad blocking while watching YouTube.

PewDie was supporting ad-free Red so the talent could get paid; his show *Scare PewDiePie* would be available on Red effective immediately, commercial free. "Ads are annoying, I get it," Kjellberg noted. He did, however, worry that the "consequences" could be "devastating" and that many would not get paid. The problem was that another informal Twitter poll by Kjellberg had revealed most people just wouldn't pay $10 a month when they could get the same content free by using ad blockers.

From the department of strange bedfellows: Pew-DiePie found his interest in ad blocking echoed by none other than Edward Snowden, who suggested in an interview with *The Intercept* that everyone should use ad blockers as a means of privacy protection, even though most of us had long since revealed our most intimate secrets to Google and Facebook, not to mention the IRS, and could never get that privacy back. But I digress.

The larger point was this: Many, many people were buzzing about or responding to ad blocking. On this score, my son, YouTube nation, and Edward Snowden were aligned. The ad blocking conversation was everywhere.

Across the aisle, in the ad-monetized media world, however, the rise of all these ad-free models was causing historic waves of chaos. Would enough people be willing to pay to avoid ads to make subscription a viable model? Could increased subscription fees ever make up for all that lost ad revenue?

In the end, it really didn't matter. It would have to. And the industry would have to adapt. Because regular people were walking away from bad ads.

Which brings us to the trillion-dollar question: Why are people turning away from advertising, and in such great numbers? Why have so many selected to sever their relationship with commercially-minded communications? A good question. To dramatize this hot mess in miniature, let's get back to my son and me, and our little bonding adventure in ad blocking.

A critical point here: The boy and I weren't out to get something, we weren't plotting to steal, like the sub-rosa file sharers of yesteryear. We weren't asking for content to be free. We weren't asking for *more*.

No, we were actually asking for *less*.

As nascent ad blockers, we were assuming a completely new, or—to be fair—an achingly old posture. We were saying *no* to being annoyed, we were saying *no* to stuff we didn't want, we were revisiting a dynamic that had always been there but that an overwhelmingly cluttered *context* had rendered untenable.

It wasn't the fault of the ad. Well, not entirely. Though the ads were often annoying, the larger problem was the swirling gyre of noise that *surrounded* the ads. Yes, it was this new context that was changing our attitude toward the content. We all had so much on our plates, anything that lessened the burden became our BFF. To paraphrase Mitt Romney, ad block adopters are people, too. We're just looking for a way to lessen the onslaught.

There was a lot of noise out there. The media business, which had bloated to historic proportions via new platforms piling up on top of old ones, was filling the world with a relentless array of content, much of it ever noisier. Many magazines had gone away, but many more things had taken their place. It was not uncommon for some Web news organizations to regularly deliver journalism—slideshows, listicles, clickbait—specifically designed to create more inventory to serve more ads, thus making themselves part of the problem, a storm surge of dubious content competing to be seen amid a historic amount of clutter, which made those unwanted ads even more annoying, a vicious cycle some had taken to calling "infobesity." And then there was the problem of fake news.

Once upon a time, when there was so much less clutter and crap, there was room for a few secondary players at the main event. Now, with so much going on, any message that announced itself as secondary actively participated in its own inconsequence. It reminded me of my old magazine days, and how affronted I used to be by random interruption. Now everyone seemed to want the ads out of the way.

It all came down to the power of less. Or, as noted by Joe Marchese, the founder of TrueX, a digital advertising company that was recently acquired by 21st Century Fox, we had a "denominator problem"—an imbalance that occurs when the total amount of content outweighs the total hours in a day, creating a dynamic in which people have no choice but to "opt out of advertising altogether." When it came to content, supply was crushing demand.

The solution? "Fewer ads."

So we blocked, and it was good.

#Toomuchness

It's funny, really, or at least a little counterintuitive. Many of us were raised to think of abundance as something *desirable*. The cornucopia, the horn of plenty, the allure of inexhaustible gifts. In practice, however ... well ... be careful what you wish for. Once we shifted the collective locus of our attention to smaller and smaller screens, abundance was no longer as appealing, and needless clutter became the enemy of useful content. Suddenly, that which is unnecessary has become outright egregious.

Yes, too much had become the issue. Toomuchness was the modern disease.

Take, for instance, the state of the TV business.

At the conclusion of 2015, FX CEO John Landgraf

gave a much-heralded speech at the Television Critics Association Summer Press Tour in which he coined the phrase "Peak TV." Landgraf pointed out, to audible gasps in the audience, that the number of scripted TV series currently available would soon pass *four hundred*. According to the KCRW blog "The Spin Off," which reported on the event, the actual number is 409. This represents an 84 percent jump from 2009, when there were "a mere 211 series" on the air, and a 484 percent jump from 2002.

The point being: *It's no longer physically possible to consume all these TV shows.* A culling would be required, and only the strong would survive. And it would be hard, too, because there were so many really great shows, like never before on the TV screen.

The novelist Don DeLillo once dismissively wrote that for most people, there are only two places: where they live and their TV set. "If a thing happens on television," he added, "we have every right to find it fascinating, whatever it is."

I'm not sure the second half of that sentence could still be uttered so facetiously. The makers of TV certainly spend a lot of time trying harder these days. And in doing so, they've encouraged a lot of it. All that good TV also makes it harder to endure ads.

It seemed that the only way for a rational person to

get a grip on this toomuchness is to compress all that content into a single feed. Some might call this metaphor an oversimplification, but today, when there's so much coming at us—from the abundance of Peak TV to Facebook, Instagram, Snapchat, and Twitter—the feed becomes our new media Main Street, the boulevard of boundless content. The feed is our overcrowded avenue of disparate interests, and we're boulevardiers, strolling along, walking briskly toward good content from creators, friends, and trusted sources and recoiling from anything that shouts or tries to sell us something unwanted or uninteresting—i.e., ads.

Ads, which had been permitted to interrupt for so long, were no longer welcome in such a world; they could no longer elbow their way into this relentless feed.

The popular podcaster Marc Maron, host of *WTF,* recently nailed this point when he went on a tirade mocking how so much marketing literally *screams* at people to garner attention. "It's like, *HEY BUDDY, OVER HERE, Tonight on CBS,*" he screamed, parodying this huckster's approach. Then, after mocking other people's ads, he switched, in the same sentence, to a live ad for "POW!-I-just-shit-my-pants Coffee" (or, as the brand actually calls itself, Just Coffee). Interesting times, indeed.

Interesting times, yes. And a time to be interesting. In the age of the Feed, the age of infobesity and Peak TV, one was compelled as never before to be entertaining

and authentic, to tell a good story, the key to being interesting.

This was something that human beings *and* marketers
alike could agree on: the power of a good story. Now
that would always be welcome; good stories were something we could never have enough of. This was the sentiment uttered by the chief marketing officer of GE, at a
recent industry conference. "Nothing," she said, "will
take the place of great storytelling."

But could advertisers even tell stories? Could brands
be interesting when they'd been trained to interrupt instead? And if they found something interesting to say,
where would they say it, given the rise of so many ad-
free platforms and all that ad-blocking technology? This
was the real conundrum: Was there even any white space
left?

Much has been made of the so-called Golden Age of
Television, and the rise of the cord cutter, but it's rarely
pointed out, even though it's so obvious, that the artistic
triumph of the small screen has paradoxically come at
the expense of advertising. It was the ability to binge-
watch great TV via platforms like iTunes, Netflix, and
of course HBO—*without* the infuriatingly tone-deaf im-
position of traditional advertising—that unleashed such
rampant creativity and attracted so much major talent to
the enterprise in the first place.

The cable channel AMC is something of an outlier in

this respect. Great programming like *Breaking Bad* and *The Walking Dead* is still broadcast *with* advertising, incredibly, for those who don't know better than to watch via the antiquated appointment TV model. But many prefer to pay to watch it when they want it, without advertising, on iTunes.

Is there any doubt which is the better way?

Unfortunately—or at least unfortunately for viewers—the ad-supported model for networks such as AMC remains far more lucrative. What do you do when the better way makes less money?

You know you're living in interesting times when this conversation, normally relegated to industry trade publications, reaches the pages of *The New Yorker.* That's exactly what happened in the fall of 2015, when Emily Nussbaum, the magazine's prickly television critic, in discussing the current exalted state of television, called advertising "TV's original sin," pointing out, quite correctly, that TV used to be incapable of competing as good art "because it was tainted" by the presence of commercials. "It was there to sell."

Yes, TV used to be about selling, a medium shaped to accommodate commercial interruption. But then one day, slowly but surely, from the first breath of HBO to the hyperventilating ambition of Netflix, everyone was suddenly bingeing on vast quantities of TV without commercials. And lo, TV was suddenly an art form.

It's a point worth emphasizing: *TV got better when advertising stopped spoiling it.*

But as I said, a lot of people still haven't shifted their habit away from linear "appointment" TV. And there are still far too many complacent brands, still helmed by unseeing marketing executives, who still believe in the old interruption model. The center will not hold.

Some networks have been making concessions to help relieve audiences from the onslaught of ads, but even these attempts might be too little too late. When NBC's *Saturday Night Live* debuted its forty-second season on October 1, 2016, in addition to new cast members and another array of hit-and-miss sketches, the iconic cultural barometer boasted, per *Variety,* 30 percent fewer ads. Whereas seventeen minutes of the ninety-minute program had previously been devoted to commercial messages, that number, according to network executives, had been reduced to a mere twelve minutes and fifteen seconds. New, too, were "branded content packages," which were apparently more tolerable to the show's putatively millennial audience than traditional spots. All told, this would improve the live viewing experience, live being something that drove tune-in and thus commanded attention. As with sports, live events still permitted commercial interruption, just as long as they were deployed judiciously. It was a victory for moderation, though it's hard to say anyone was cheering.

In the end, mere moderation just won't cut it. It's just a matter of time before the status quo gives way and all ads are eaten alive by blockers—just as soon as TV ads are as easy to block as Internet advertising.

How do I know this with such certainty? Because life is just better without ads. Don't believe me? Here's a fun thought experiment: Ask anyone who doesn't know about ad blocking or ad-free TV what they'd say if they knew that, for a little more money, they could watch Walter White or all those decomposing walkers without commercials, without all those annoying interruptions, and you won't need a subscription to *The New Yorker* to see that the unloved thirty-second television commercial can't last forever, and that it's likely to become extinct almost everywhere content is enthusiastically consumed. The traditional TV ad is, to be crass, ultimately headed for hospice care. The only question, again to be blunt, is how long it will take to die.

Meanwhile, Web and mobile ads are also doomed because Web and mobile content is also much better without traditional ads. (This might fly in the face of Facebook's recently reported $3.4 billion in mobile advertising revenue, which, along with Google, now accounts for over 80 percent of the overall ad business, according to *Mashable*. But you could argue, as many have, that Facebook is essentially the operating system of the Internet, even if they exaggerate the amount of time people spend on the platform. In an ad-supported landscape in which there is Facebook and everybody else, Facebook gets its own advertising reality distortion field, which I will return to shortly.)

In the end, the agent of death will be the customer. Remember: They're always right.

But wait. Again you say, *I still keep seeing ads.* What gives? To which I respond, *Keep watching.* For even the most obdurate doubter can't deny that ads are quietly disappearing like peripheral characters on *Lost.* Take, for instance, the streaming TV service Hulu.

During that same crazy summer of 2015, Hulu— which had long been packed with pre-roll ads— introduced, with great fanfare, its new *commercial-free option,* cleverly named the "No Commercials" plan. This new Hulu model would save viewers from the torment of unskippable advertising for a mere $11.99 a month.

The CEO of Hulu, who didn't seem especially happy about the news, reluctantly noted that "you can divide people into two categories: 'ad avoiders' and 'ad acceptors,'" which essentially meant *wolves* and *sheep,* or perhaps *smart* and *stupid,* a not especially charitable take on humanity, not to mention a potentially suicidal reading of the TV marketplace (as if anyone would accept un-skippable ads given the slightest affordable alternative). A few months later, unsurprisingly, Hulu announced that it would be winding down its free, ad-supported offering and move fully to a paid subscription model. Shortly thereafter, the "old media" people at CBS announced their own ad-free subscription service, according to *Recode*.

But enough about TV and the Web. That's of course not the only place we see ads. What fate, industry folk wondered that fateful summer, would befall ads in maga-zines and newspapers in this new age? Could it get any worse? How long until consumers addicted to ad block-ing just said no there as well? Okay, sure, such technol-ogy is obviously not possible in print, which is rapidly losing audience anyway, but very doable to a publica-tion's digital incarnation (vide my *New York Times* ex-periment).

A harsher critic might have argued that the more likely outcome is that the physical magazine and news-paper will eventually just fade away (except perhaps for a few critical titles), à la what happened to fax machines and VCRs—and that the death of magazines and news-papers will take the entire print advertising business with it, except for outliers who make something really special.

And what of radio? Was radio even worth discussing?

Apparently, many people still listened to terrestrial radio, a platform often denigrated for its especially terrible ads, from which there was presently no escape, but which surely was not endearing itself to listeners who were increasingly disinclined to put up with something they didn't ask for and who had more alternatives than ever.

And what about our friend Howard Stern, whose satellite radio model required people to pay to listen? Why not ask Howard Stern himself if people would prefer *his* show without the ads, or if they'd be willing to pay an even higher subscription fee to SiriusXM if an ad-free model existed? Would Stern's listeners embrace a platform that allowed them to enjoy his show better without ads? Or maybe Stern could simply instruct his advertisers, Larry Page style, to be less annoying. And while we're at it, it's worth noting that this very same concern had been raised in 1938, by the Ford executive William J. Cameron, who pointed out that "radio gave birth to impertinent advertising." Some problems just take time to reach critical mass.

As with their rivals in terrestrial radio, music streaming services like Spotify and Pandora would continue to present a split personality in the form of their ad-supported free and ad-free paid models (unless one split the difference and downloaded the Adblocker for Spotify app for $4.99), creating a new digital divide of haves and have-nots, and ostensibly supporting a dialectic in which the only people left who'll have to hear ads are the economically challenged who can't afford not to.

And what about billboards, those massive ads that besmirch cities and highways? In the industry, we refer to this channel as out-of-home. It also refers to the giant posters, some static, some digital, that create the oscillating bright lights we tend to associate with places like Times Square and Tokyo.

Would these messages go away, too, as depicted in that *AdAge* cover? Would Times Square ever go dark? Probably not, or at least not as certainly as other forms of advertising, because OOH was perhaps the last monolithic form of communication, resistant to time shifting or the whims of the individual. A single person, no matter how motivated, still couldn't turn off the lights. We'll get back to out-of-home shortly, and Citibank's genius take on how to make it suck less and become useful.

Yes, much was changing in Adland, and change was happening the way change always does, in fits and starts—rapid historic shifts in certain circles, elsewhere an absolute resistance to progress. But a new paradigm was crystallizing for anyone with the slightest sense of pattern recognition. The key obstacles were the status quo and the incumbent media industry's cracklike addiction to ad revenue, like someone with a gluten allergy incapable of parting company with pizza.

And then there was the small matter of figuring out an entirely new business model to make the relationship between media and marketing still work for regular people.

Which brings us to a time-horizon vs. cost-benefit calculation. There's a lot of money to be lost—and made—from the end of traditional advertising. Just how long this shift takes will depend on where you sit on the value chain.

It's coming. The question is *when*. But how long will the incumbents fight back the rising waters of doom? That remains to be seen. Keepers of the old guard—network television sales execs, advertising holding company CEOs, publishers—will tell you that the impact of blocking and rumors of the death of traditional advertising are exaggerated.

With all due respect, I'm afraid they're on the wrong side of history, caught between the present and the future and hanging on for dear life until retirement.

I'd say the end of advertising as we know it is somewhere between five minutes and five years. That said, in the interest of being prepared, I'd buy the black suit tomorrow.

I might even go so far as to say that the last century of advertising has been a massive historic anomaly—that this extinction event was always in the forecast.

One day, we'll look back on the fact that we *forced*

people to watch ads with the same incredulity we reserve for, say, smoking cigarettes or wearing fedoras. Perhaps the more enlightened brands should start thinking about reparations.

Use It or Lose It: So What Do We Do with All That Money?

If the traditional role of advertising is in serious jeopardy—and it is—the good news, depending on your point of view, is that the money behind it isn't.

Once the ad as we know it is eradicated, where will all those ad dollars go? Because here is perhaps the most intriguing point: Advertising *budgets* aren't shrinking; those dollars will still be spent. What will change is the product itself and the places where traditional advertising once appeared.

This would require some imagination. It would require creativity. And it would require putting authenticity ahead of artifice. But before we move forward, let's look back.

TV ads represent 38% of all US ad spend. It is such a HUGE number. To think that this money will disappear is crazy. Where will it go??

—@alexiskold, managing director of TechStars,
the startup accelerator

Most people who know anything about the modern advertising business tend to know what they know from watching *Mad Men,* the brilliant AMC series that ran from 2007 to 2015. As someone who served as a real-life Roger Sterling for nearly a decade, during perhaps the most tumultuous period in advertising history, I can say from experience that *Mad Men* pretty much got it all right, and that much of the dynamic remains the same—minus the three-martini lunches. What changed was the world around us, in ways that would have made Roger's and Don Draper's heads spin.

As *Mad Men* often depicted it, here's how the modern advertising business *used* to work: A client had something to sell; an ad agency was hired to craft a clever way to sell it. I oversimplify, but only a little. The crystallization of this process was invariably a commercial, which traditionally resulted in something you saw on television, or in a magazine or newspaper, or heard on the radio.

This modus operandi is generally referred to as the Command & Control era of advertising, a golden age (for some, at least), when mass audiences were held captive by the three (!) television channels, a dozen periodicals, and the local radio station.

Seen through a nostalgic gray flannel lens, it was a simpler time: One's media options were few, and the ads—the classic thirty-second spot, the print insertion, the DJ "live read"—were part of the equation, whether you liked it or not. Given that there wasn't much else competing for mind share, no one really knew any better, and the viewing audiences' inability to express outrage was misconstrued as permission. Interruption and disruption became the reigning model, a series of arbitrary insertions rudely shoved into whatever you were doing. And so it went, rinse and repeat, from the Civil War until Al Gore invented the Internet.

Suddenly, as noted earlier, the business of making the thing that sells the thing got a lot more complicated.

Were he toiling on Madison Avenue today, Don Draper would have a hard time navigating the complexity of the current advertising landscape. Beyond the aforementioned array of blocking technologies, advertising must now compete with, in no particular order, massive media fragmentation, mobile mass adoption, cord cutters, self-quantification, selfies, podcasts, a million apps, a zillion video games, endlessly proliferating social media platforms, the golden age of TV (made binge-worthy, as noted, by the absence of ads), the hegemonic power of texting, the chimerical pursuit of "inbox zero," and dozens more dopamine-stimulating bits and bobs that drive the economy of unprecedented abundance that is modern life.

Think about it: When traditional advertising was first invented, there were sixteen or so waking hours in a day.

That baseline hasn't changed, but the number of things frenetically competing for our attention at any given moment has, we all know, increased exponentially. What Michael Schudson, author of *Advertising, the Uneasy Persuasion,* called "the customer's information environment" has been officially overrun. In the Command & Control years, there was room for advertising, or certainly more room than there is now, even as viewers of yore still recognized it as the price of admission.

Today, however, when every free second is spoken for, there is literally no room left for *anything* that is inherently secondary. Today's viewer has developed a binary system for evaluating content (yes/no/yes/no/no/no). That which has zero value—i.e., advertising (*nooooo*)—is instantaneously dismissed with neurological precision.

Snapchat, which is new to this game, recently revealed that many users stopped watching its video ads after three seconds, which sounds to me like two seconds too long.

In most channels, the ad more often than not is either uncalled for or invisible. If it's not flat-out ignored, much advertising is being left-swiped away, like a massive version of Tinder. Just watch any millennial consuming media in real time, especially on a mobile device. Cluttered context is shoving out uninvited content.

If only more brands would take heed.

It's a pity, really, because this onslaught of noise doesn't make people any less interested in buying things. We're just much less interested in noise we don't need.

Given how much things have changed, it's instructive to revisit the late David Ogilvy, philosopher king of Madison Avenue, who once famously said he didn't think of advertising as a form of entertainment, let alone an art form, but rather a medium of information. "I want you to buy the product," he proclaimed, explaining the ad man's role in the universe. Today, a medium of information is obliged to be entertaining, lest it be discarded in the din.

Ogilvy would hardly recognize today's world, a place where the pure information tonnage is so overwhelming that the uninteresting or overtly commercial is a medium of irritation. The fact is, Ogilvy's emphasis on selling and his de-emphasis on entertainment came to represent the worst ideals of the advertising industry, classic "bad-vertising" that now finds itself being asphyxiated.

I've been reading Ogilvy a lot recently, mostly ironically. He often spoke about distinguishing "the eternal verities of advertising from its passing fads." Sorry, Sir David, but I don't think we're facing a fad this time. It's over, baby. All good things must come to an end. You got very, very rich, but your progeny produced so much crap that the grand comeuppance is at long last upon us.

I'd like to think the irony would not be lost on Ogilvy. When he started in 1949, the ad landscape was being wildly disrupted by the advent of television, which had emerged as "the most potent medium for selling most products." Ogilvy, always thinking ahead, assumed that more disruptive media would appear (and that billboards would be abolished). But by 1983, when he published his seminal *Ogilvy on Advertising,* the master had come to the conclusion that since nothing of any great significance had changed the way advertising was made since the birth of TV five decades earlier, nothing ever would.

It's rather amazing just how wrong he was, and how much has changed since the eighties, the last unassailable hurrah for advertising agencies. Sadly, David Ogilvy didn't live to see the World Wide Web, as they used to call it. It's hard to imagine *Ogilvy on Internet Advertising,* let alone wrapping his mind around a $700,000 sponsored selfie filter on Snapchat, or measuring the conversion lift of promoted tweets.

But enough with David Ogilvy. Like so many philosopher kings, history proved him wrong. He thought nothing would ever change, and then some kid named Henrik Aasted Sørensen invented ad blocking, and Ogilvy's entire kingdom all went to hell.

Patient Zero

Not long ago, in one of its many articles on the rise of ad blocking since the summer of 2015, *The Wall Street Journal* acknowledged that blocking behavior, "once relegated to the geek crowd ... was hitting the mainstream." Ad blocking had suddenly scaled to the point of commanding mainstream news coverage, the marketing equivalent of Occupy Wall Street (Inhibit Madison Avenue?), but the story implied that the phenomenon had begun as revenge by some nerds.

So who, exactly, started ad blocking in the first place?

It turns out that a geek did indeed invent this after all. A Danish college kid. Yes, a good portion of the ad-blocking revolution can be blamed on a single European university student named Henrik Aasted Sørensen, who in 2002, according to a rare interview in *Business Insider,* wrote the original AdBlock source code when he was a freelancer in Copenhagen "as a way to distract him from his university work."

Sørensen's original software simply made ads invisible; it didn't actually stop ads from being downloaded, which is what happens now. Sørensen open-sourced his code, as kids are wont to do, and suddenly hundreds of geeks were grokking his idea and expanding its reach and intensity.

By 2006, AdBlock was acquired by a German software developer with the Bond villain name of Wladimir

Palant, who then started a company called Eyeo, advancing Sørensen's original code as AdBlock Plus. This is around the time that the extortion element kicked in, as AdBlock Plus begins to charge certain publishers for the privilege of unblocking their ads.

Though Sørensen claims to dislike the extortionist tendencies of the players who have expanded and commercialized his code, he likes "the wider goal of developing non-intrusive ads." Like everyone else, he wants a "less cluttered and noisy" world. Which is why I like to think of Sørensen as the ACLU of ad blocking, motivated by good intentions, either heroic or naive, depending on where you sit in the food chain.

Perhaps it isn't as iconic a tale as Mark Zuckerberg in his Harvard dorm, but there's clearly something charming about the origin story of ad blocking. There's also something charming about how one man's tiny innovation changed mass behavior. As *The New York Times* pointed out, young adults, my son included, are now gleefully embracing ad-skipping apps the way an earlier generation embraced the Hula Hoop.

"Everything you know about advertising—chuck it," said industry icon Laura Desmond, the former head of one of the world's biggest ad-buying companies, trying to make sense of ad-block nation. "It's a completely different world and game with millennials."

The Kids Are Alright

The ads that don't appeal to me are a waste of my time.

—Daniel Perel, 26, typical millennial, quoted in
The New York Times, September 28, 2015

Hey Ads, People Are Just Not That Into You

—headline in *The Wall Street Journal,*
October 2, 2015

Not long ago I was walking down a NoHo sidestreet when I came across an ad I liked. The ad was on a poster, a so-called wild posting, a freshly glued piece of oak tag with a block of striking large-type copy that stood out like a nude body on the street. The ad was for a new social network called Ello, which I had never heard of, have never used, and likely never will, but I responded to its bold Gen Z attitude.

It should be mentioned that I don't have the slightest association with this company, nor do I care much about them or think they're particularly successful. Nevertheless, I found what they were saying especially astute. It felt as if they were onto something, possibly way ahead of their time, and, as with anyone new who shares one's point of view, I admired how much they'd apparently been reading my mind.

The ad, ironically, was about Ello not having ads.

"Beautiful & ad-free," began the company manifesto in aggressive 45-point type. How interesting to conflate beauty with the absence of ads. The copy continued:

> Your social network is owned by adver-
> tisers. Every post you share, every friend
> you make and every link you follow is
> tracked, recorded and converted into
> data. Advertisers buy your data so they
> can show you more ads. You are the
> product that's bought and sold. We be-
> lieve there is a better way.

Then I realized the people at Ello and I were actually not aligned. These guys cared about privacy. I just cared about pollution.

Yes, Ello was using Facebook as its stalking horse. They were flogging the tedious assumption that Facebook, the three-hundred-pound gorilla in this attack ad, was using data for nefarious purposes. I say "tedious" because everyone knows Facebook leverages all our personal data and yet people keep using it, privacy be damned. Anyone who has ever used Facebook, or Gmail for that matter, has surely known the creepy feeling of being followed around the Web by advertisers who seem to possess an intimate familiarity with our private habits.

And yet no one really seems to care. We have a handful of watchdog groups fighting for our privacy, which is laudable. But let's get real. We're talking about a *social* network, after all, a canvas on which one is applauded for sharing inappropriate bikini and bachelor party pics. Discretion is not the better part of the social grid, and concerns about the loss of privacy on a platform conceived to encourage oversharing seem, IMHO, to be misplaced, to put it mildly.

To be clear, the defense of privacy is not a factor in the coming end of advertising. People, or at least people like Edward Snowden, may worry that Internet publishers are sharing their likes and dislikes with advertisers, but this, I would argue, isn't anywhere as worrisome to regular people as the need to get away from bad, unwelcome ads.

Recently, CNBC ran a graphic that seemed to prove this point. In trying to break down the reasons why so many young people were blocking ads, they stipulated that privacy represented the motivation behind only 17 percent of people who were blocking ads. The larger percentage of blockers just didn't want to be interrupted.

So, sure, privacy matters.

But not being annoyed matters more.

It was time for advertisers to realize that young people, not to mention people of all ages, really, really don't like being annoyed. And ads, almost always, were annoying. There is nothing beautiful, let alone useful, not to mention authentic, about being interrupted, distracted, or annoyed by something you didn't choose to see.

Banner Blindness

By the way, it just so happened I'd come across that Ello ad during the week of the twentieth anniversary of the so-called banner ad, the highly polarizing unit that in two decades had turned the ad-supported Web into a sea of ugly clutter and frequent exasperation.

This was an important anniversary. When the Web was first invented, advertising was simply not part of the equation. Later, as traditional publishers began to see that the Net was not a fad but rather a massive disruptive force—the first new media platform to arrive in half a century, something that threatened TV the way TV had threatened radio—there was a need for a metaphor that would help early users envision monetization strategies.

Search was simple and could easily be tied to customers who would pay to own keywords. A Web "page" was also a simple and familiar construct to get one's head around. And if the Internet had pages, well, then it was just like a newspaper or a magazine, and could accommodate adjacencies, those aforementioned arbitrary placements, in which a secondary thing (i.e., an ad) was put next to a primary (i.e., a story)—the very model that I used to ignore as a magazine guy.

Thus was created the so-called banner ad or "display advertising," the unit to the right of the Web page, the annoying box that still follows those of us who haven't downloaded ad blockers around the Web.

But here's the problem: Twenty years later, as many thinkers have pointed out, it turns out that these ads are not "Web native." They do not belong there; they don't fit in an ontological sense. They were only there because a small group of people had decided to jam them in, because they could, and because there had to be a way to monetize the thing, which was fair.

But just because you can do something doesn't mean you should; the first way to make money isn't necessarily the right one. And twenty years later, the world was finally catching up. There would need to be a better way, something better than annoying banner ads, or everyone would block them into obscurity. And forcing people to endure them, as so many desperate publishers were doing, was most certainly not the solution.

These intrusions were exactly what I had hoped the Ello team was setting out to stop.

So when I understood what Ello was on about, as they say in England, what had put the company's knickers in a twist, I realized that our values were not aligned.

They were not even close. "Beautiful and ad-free" seemed like such a paradisiacal construct, such an inviting environment, that my attention had been piqued. But Ello turned out to be just a bunch of privacy advocates playing the paranoia card.

Now, I had *thought* Ello was proposing something that *people really want to see:* a beautiful, ad-free planet in which advertising as we know it is no more, because context has rendered it unwelcome.

It's All Good

Which brings us back to ad blocking, which I have come to regard, heretically, as the greatest thing that has ever happened to the advertising industry. To me, its importance cannot be underestimated. I see blocking as the latest in a long string of technological innovations that have positively reshaped human behavior, somewhere between the Gutenberg press and the typewriter.

Yes, ad blocking represents a massive disruptive change. At long last, we have at our disposal a technology that allows people to take matters directly into their own hands, self-selecting a world without ads. And make no mistake, people are voting, voting with their phones, tablets, and desktops, voting in large numbers.

Once upon a time, the only way to block an ad was to go to the bathroom during the break, to protest by peeing. Now there was an app for that! America had spoken. The rise of mass ad blocking felt more like . . . a *movement*.

Actually, long before TiVo and somewhere after the bathroom break, there was another ad-blocking technology: the remote control. As harmless as that plastic brick feels today, the mass adoption of the handheld zapper was once considered just as threatening to Madison Avenue as ad blocking. Actually, one could argue, as *BuzzFeed* founder Jonah Peretti recently suggested when the subject came up at a private media conference, that the original ad-blocking technology was "the human neck," in the sense that TV-watching people have long been habituated to simply look down, or away, when a bad ad comes up. One could argue that the VCR, which first allowed people to fast-forward through commercials, was another critical blow.

But back in the summer of 2015, when this was all new, some still refused to see the big picture.

Things reached a fever pitch of sorts on September 28, 2015, the start of the twelfth annual "Advertising Week" in NYC, when both *The Wall Street Journal* and *The New York Times* weighed in with more or less the exact same story. The pope and the president were in town, the annual United Nations General Assembly was under way, but many of the world's most powerful media and marketing execs could speak of nothing else except this troubling cri de coeur.

"Ad Blocking Is a Hot Topic for Marketing Executives," kvetched the *Journal,* noting the widespread wringing of hands and heartburn that ad blocking had wrought. The story claimed that the explosive growth of the digital advertising business was now under attack. And, in the final paragraph, it blamed all this indigestion on media companies for larding their products with ads, "thereby annoying consumers," echoing Google's Larry Page and reinforcing the doomed-if-you-do-doomed-if-you-don't dilemma facing ad-supported media sellers at the moment.

But this time, the solution, which had been proposed for years, was finally being heard. If ad blocking was here to stay, the only logical conclusion was that marketers would actually have to rethink ads.

Meanwhile, over at the NFL, it was business as usual.

Deflategate?

I think the NFL is ten years away from an implosion. When you've got a good thing and you get greedy, it always, always, always, always turns on you.

—entrepreneur Mark Cuban to ESPN, 2014

There remains one major exception complicating the coming end of traditional advertising: live sports, which, unlike every other form of media now facing historic disruption, seems to have been specifically conceived to accommodate commercials and thus perpetuate the status quo.

There is no live sport more successful than the NFL in exploiting this felicitous structural advantage (at least until the good people at AdBlock find a way), and no ad-fueled media business is safer. Or as a recent headline in *AdAge* put it, "TV Is Now Merely a Delivery System for the NFL." Which is why all the supremely expensive ad space for the 2016 Super Bowl, which we shall discuss in a moment, would be sold out by November 2015.

But even on the exalted NFL stage, there's an interesting tension that gets odder with each passing season: On any given Sunday, at least during the regular sixteen-game season, viewers are subjected every few minutes to a tedious carousel of car, fast food, and retirement commercials, most of which are so stultifyingly bad that the subtext is "Perhaps you should pee now."

It's amazing how resistant this model is to the disruptive forces influencing change everywhere else. But it's foolish to think such a delicate truce will last forever, even for the seemingly invincible NFL, before a new ad-blocking platform concusses it into a coma. Maybe that's why the league saw a surprising 11 percent drop in viewership, according to *The Wall Street Journal,* at the start of the 2016 season.

But wait. The end of the NFL season brings the great white whale of advertising: the Super Bowl, the lone day a year that Americans all unite in their love for advertising rather than thinking up ways to avoid it, and Madison Avenue redeems itself.

Weird. For a mere $5 million for thirty seconds of airtime—the going rate for a Super Bowl spot according to *The Wall Street Journal*—the world's top brands set out to produce their own mini golden age of television, in some instances blowing their entire annual budget in the hope of striking viral gold.

It's a great spectacle, and though mostly futile, one that often results in fantastic content that also happens to be advertising, work that is sometimes so good that people discuss it at the watercooler the following day. But then, having seemingly learned nothing, the industry reverts to its time-tested model of serving us inconsequential dreck throughout the entire next season, until the big game returns yet again.

It's hard to imagine *Breaking Bad* getting away with such a terrible batting average, to mix sports metaphors. This, too, shall not last.

Yes, the Super Bowl is a world unto itself, with its own rules and regulations. And that game and other "big tent" live events—the World Series, the Oscars, the Grammys, anything involving Caitlyn Jenner or a Kardashian—will likely, for better or worse, perpetuate the existence of traditional advertising until the end of time.

Meanwhile, advertising that *doesn't* happen during the Super Bowl will increasingly seem like a high-profile anachronism. For many people, all those tedious breaks just aren't tolerable anymore.

The irony is that the Super Bowl approach actually provides a useful lesson: In a world in which we are drowning in noise, any content, whether it's advertising or serial crime dramas, must be qualitatively superior to be appreciated, and that doesn't always require a huge budget.

The most important thing is to be excellent, interesting, authentic, or useful.

To be the thing, not the thing that sells the thing.

That's fantastic news for creative people, who specialize in the stuff.

Thanks to toomuchness, creativity, once exclusively the province of poets, has suddenly become a business imperative.

Pattern Recognition

Every fall, the Association of National Advertisers, one of the largest trade organizations representing the interests of Madison Avenue and the brands that employ it, hosts a conference rather boldly called "Masters of

Marketing." The conference toggles back and forth each year between such hotbeds of innovation as Orlando and Scottsdale, regularly drawing the biggest chief marketing officers on the planet, along with four thousand more marketing executives keen to schmooze and booze, eat rubber chicken, and prognosticate on the future of advertising. It's long been a must-attend for industry potentates.

In attendance during a muggy week in late October 2015 were such iconic incumbents as Pepsi, Audi, and GE, who presented their communication strategies alongside such disruptive newcomers as Airbnb, Lyft, and Mashable (which subsequently seemed to go through something of a collapse). ANA can be fun. There's always a golf or tennis tournament, a mock casino night, and entertainment of a certain stature. In 2015, Seal entertained the troops. A few years ago, the industry stretched a bit and lured Tony Danza to tickle the ivories. But this year there was a very different feeling in the air. The golf course was half empty.

The ANA's mission is to "share the latest insights, inventions and best practices in an atmosphere conducive to collaboration." In the past, the posture of the conference has been rather self-congratulatory, bordering on complacent. Though there are always knotty issues of some consequence plaguing the ad industry, this near-trillion-dollar behemoth tends to exude an atmosphere of invulnerable bonhomie.

This year, however, there was definitely a different vibration to be detected. Much of it started when ANA CEO Bob Liodice issued the following proclamation: "We must swallow our pride," he said, "and recognize that ad blocking represents consumer *outrage*."

What followed was a series of presentations from the people who control the advertising budgets of some of the largest brands on the planet. Some of them, without naming names, were clearly responsible for that outrage, and had clearly not heard their leader's message.

As the presentations unfolded, one could detect, perhaps for the first time in a long time, a dawning sense from all the big-time marketers that the ground was shifting beneath their feet. Many increasingly saw their primary job requirement, which had always been about driving sales, shifting to the more pressing responsibility of *not outraging consumers*.

Even more important, one detected a sense that there might actually be a correlation between these two ideas.

To tell the truth, it had long been gospel among a minority of marketers that brand love equaled brand sales. *If people liked how you communicated, they might like your product, and maybe even buy it, or buy more of it!* But there had long been a louder constituency, often backed by data rather than humanity, who said, *Screw that, our job is to hit Joe Consumer over the head with a relentless sales pitch until he empties his wallet from sheer fatigue.* Could the power be shifting from the quants to the quals?

There were signs everywhere. Dunkin Donuts' CMO said the company was now all about value and utility; for example, it had recently partnered with the social navigation app Waze, using location-based marketing, to offer discounts based on a traveler's proximity to a store. Fox, for instance, announced it was "testing ways to limit its commercial load on its digital platforms." One such example was *MasterChef Junior*, an entirely commercial-free partnership with the California Milk Advisory Board (commercial-free as long as viewers "interacted" with a 60-second ad at the start of the show, but thoughtful nevertheless). Myriad marketers were striding on-stage to proclaim to their peers that they were sincerely trying to do better, and pledging fealty to all putative blockers out there to No. Longer. Be. Annoying. It felt a bit like an AA meeting, all this sheepish oversharing. Call it Advertisers Anonymous.

"It's incumbent on us to find better answers and fix the relationship," said one marketer.

To which I would say *duh*.

Even the mainstream beer industry, which had a long

tradition of amusing consumers via clever advertising, but which had recently, like an arthritic power hitter, fallen into a slump of especially annoying work, was rethinking its model.

According to *The Wall Street Journal,* the rise of craft beers had created a "sense of urgency" inside the marketing machine at AB/InBev, the giant conglomerate. InBev had fired its fourth ad agency in four years. Bud, Miller, and Coors were looking for new, less annoying creative, too.

The head of Anheuser-Busch marketing said that his company was no longer "doing breakthrough work," citing, as an example of what *not* to do, a campaign in which a twentysomething man played a life-sized game of Pac-Man. The ad was dismissed as hedonistic and "focused on live for today, not for tomorrow." The solution, it seemed, was to be "clever and witty" rather than "sophomoric."

I would respectfully submit that the only real solution was to firmly put the consumer first, and maybe reconsider the rampant use of the word "consumer," or just stop reflexively assuming that he or she was consuming something. Maybe they were just human beings. And for Bud to begin by asking itself a more existential question: Can any advertising be appreciated, rather than just highly annoying, in a world of too much?

The Corrections

Can I just fire everyone?

—Roger Sterling, *Mad Men*

It is generally agreed that the annual figure spent on global advertising now exceeds $600 billion, more than twice the GDP of Norway. Others, from *AdAge* to *eMarketer,* estimate that the correct figure is actually closer to $1.2 trillion, which is about the size of the GDP of Mexico. These are mind-boggling numbers. Given that the bulk of this money is mostly devoted to producing crap, and that at least half of it is generally agreed to be ineffective by the very people who make or commission it, one might even call it a catastrophe.

But all is not lost.

There's another way to think about the rise of ad blocking. Could this secular change in the way people relate to advertising instead be a Correction, with a capital C?

Could this be a Darwinian moment for media, a time when only the fittest will survive and mutation is necessary for the species to continue? Is this the kaboom that had yet to be heard? Was the rise of ad blocking just a metaphor for the water that recedes before the devastating tsunami? Is it possible that the entire trillion-dollar global advertising business, as most people understand it (minus live sports), is in a more precarious position than a piñata? Is it actually in existential trouble?

I certainly think so.

Can it be that this unloved industry, which has flourished for more than a century, making so many people so much money, the world's biggest remora fish, is finally facing the repercussions of years of mediocrity and disregard, and that it is now careening toward obsolescence if not outright extinction?

And if so, why? And if millions of consumers, which is to say *regular people,* are embracing technology to avoid ads, if a legion of laypeople have finally seen Paris from the farm, doesn't that constitute a revolution, albeit one in slow motion? Is the adpocalypse truly upon us, deadly real rather than just an easy pun? And what will the new world look like once the ad-eating zombies have run amok?

A wise man once said, "Convenience trumps hubris," and smarter words have never been spoken. Once technology raises a tide that results in a superior user experience, it cannot be reversed. Just as the record business (for those old enough to remember) went from LPs to cassettes to CDs to digital files, could ad blocking force Madison Avenue to move from annoying and useless pollution to telling stories that people might actually want to hear, or to being an appreciated and welcome utility?

Isn't it time to try a little harder?

Tipping Point

Sometimes it's useful to look at how other industries undo years of entrenched habit. It certainly happened in the restaurant business.

In October 2015, around the time that Adland was first getting roiled by ad blocking, the wildly successful New York restaurateur Danny Meyer—who is perhaps best known for creating Shake Shack, but whose true influence comes from his role as longtime owner/operator of Gramercy Tavern and Union Square Café, among other extremely successful luxury dining establishments—decided that he was eradicating the ancient habit of *tipping*. It wasn't as big as *Playboy* dropping nude pictures, which happened the same week, but it was a pretty historic moment nonetheless.

Effective immediately, Meyer would implement a no-tip policy. The tip slot on your check would vanish, the tip jar would be tossed into the trash. In one fell swoop, he was getting rid of an antiquated, arbitrary, and mostly annoying policy that had been around for years and thus was assumed to be irrevocable.

Meyer had spoken—one would still pay as much, but the tip would now simply be absorbed into the bill, separating the noise from the signal, making life so much easier. But the cynical media had questions. For instance: "Will the restaurant industry and political leaders listen?" As with any secular change, some would, and some wouldn't.

Either way, it's the wrong question. Industry and political leaders do not have a choice. See Paris, farm, etc. As noted, that proverbial genie had wriggled out of the bottle. The fact is, a meal without the tedium of having to calculate a tip at its conclusion is simply a better user experience for the consumer.

There is no way that the tipping *process* adds value to any diner's life, but most of us have just accepted tipping as the way it is. Sure, giving a tip might afford a diner some sense of control or a way to comment on the service, but the content itself—a math moment usually complicated by alcohol—was never particularly "native" to the actual meal. Now here was Meyer, disrupting a process that had seemed intractable. And no one would be the poorer: The tip money would simply be added to the bill. No one was getting off any cheaper; the reward for good service would still find its way to the service provider's pocket. The big difference: It would no longer be annoying. Twitter was quickly awash with applause.

Following the ethos of Jeff Bezos, Meyer *had chosen to focus on the needs of the customer,* the human being in the center of the equation. He had used his imagination and applied a little creativity to change something that was broken, instead of sticking with the status quo like so many players in Adland. This was always the right decision. Innovation that embraces such logic almost always wins.

The only question is how long it takes.

Meanwhile, back in the media business, the battle raged on. Things got weirder still in 2015 when embattled Yahoo CEO Marissa Mayer joined the pot-calling-the-kettle-black chorus by telling an industry crowd at Advertising Week, "Better ads will stop people from blocking Web ads." Here was yet another media executive making a point—like tipping, being annoying was a bad idea—that should have been obvious, despite the potentially self-destructive implications for her business.

Unfortunately, as noted, it's not just the bad ads that are the issue.

Had I had the chance to talk to Ms. Mayer back then, I would have repeated my previous point: It's not just the bad ads. It's what's around them that's part of the problem, too. As noted, when there's too much, when we find ourselves collectively ducking the denominator problem, when we're all suffering from *infobesity,* when people are rising up and creating or embracing technology that makes it easier to stop the onslaught, maybe we all ought to do *less,* do better, and focus on adding something useful, rather than just making more *more.*

Yahoo perfectly illustrates the #toomuchness problem. The company has invested—some might use a less generous verb—millions and millions of dollars producing very expensive *editorial* content, content that few people seem especially passionate about. Essentially, Mayer started a bunch of Web magazines.

Ironically, Yahoo made this huge content investment so it could monetize those Web magazines no one wanted nor needed with islands of advertising, thus bringing into the world more bad ads of the sort that people increasingly will be able to block.

And so in the perfect media and marketing microcosm that is Yahoo, we have on our hands what appears to be a massive exercise in inconsequence. Or, if you prefer, a circle jerk, in which there's just more *stuff,* if not necessarily better stuff. More stories, but rarely superior to the output of other storytellers—and a lot more ads, which are almost always annoying. Seen in that light, ad blocking makes a great deal of sense. (What Yahoo's pending new owner, Verizon, makes of all this, besides more advertising, remains to be seen.)

Yes, there could be no going back. *The New York Times* and Yahoo, not to mention everything else on the Internet, as Howard Stern rightly noticed, were simply better without all that trash.

The Internet was not lacking in content. It was lacking in *restraint*.

And now consumers were rising up to shut off the things that added nothing.

It's Been a Long Time Coming, but a Change Is Gonna Come

The Facebook is cool, that's what it's got going for it. You don't want to ruin it with ads, because ads aren't cool.

—from a fictitious (if highly plausible) conversation between Mark Zuckerberg and Sean Parker in the film *The Social Network*, 2012

Sometime in the fall of 2015, the Internet Advertising Bureau, the trade organization tasked with codifying Web ads, the same group that claimed ad blocking would tear down the global economy, pulled an about-face, capping off a truly crazy year, and issued a mea culpa regarding its position on ad blocking.

The subtext was: It's not you, it's us. This was not "highway robbery" by a bunch of tech geeks, as was the organization's previous position. Instead, the IAB suggested, ad blocking was the consequence of years and years of bad advertising. "We messed up," the organization said in a statement. As a result, the IAB tried to make amends, to the best of its limited ability: It issued a new standard for better Internet advertising.

Now *that* was sure to get Howard Stern and a million other angry Americans to stop blocking ads.

Still, it was nice of them to try. And they'd certainly come to the right conclusion. But what if it was too little too late, anyway? And while we're asking the big questions, here's another one:

Did online ads even work, anyway?

Most people in the business of Internet advertising would say *Of course they do*. But what did that response actually mean when one set out to unpack it? What did we mean by an ad's ability to "work"?

Back in Don Draper's day, it was fashionable among ad men to quip that fifty percent of advertising didn't work—but no one could say for sure which half. Today, we know with chilling certitude that a de minimis number of people actually click on Internet advertising. The average response rate is less than .02 percent, according to various sources and industry insiders. That's pretty bad. How amusing: Digital ad technology, once thought to be the future of the industry, turned out to be its mortician.

The problem is that a bad ad is a bad ad no matter where it appears. The big boys at Facebook, borne aloft by their vast audiences and bottomless caches of big data, have made advertising measurable and addressable, more science than art, and that's great. But the not-so-dirty little secret is that online advertising's general effectiveness, not to mention its value to society, hasn't improved much at all, and quite possibly has gotten much, much worse. It may be digital, but junk mail is still junk mail.

Then again, when you're Facebook and have a billion users, .02 percent is still a big number, so many call their ads a success. Maybe all is well after all. Go figure, especially if the *only* thing you care about is scale.

But if you forget about big numbers for a moment and just look at it as a human being, that pathetic response rate raises some complicated, perhaps even epistemological, questions. What on earth does it mean, what kind of riddle is being posed, when people are essentially blocking something without any ad-blocking technology?

In January 2016, Facebook put out a public statement acknowledging that even they have some anxiety about the rapid spread of ad blocking, according to *Business Insider*. Apparently, ad blocking affects Facebook "from time to time."

By August 2016, however, Facebook had changed its tune. That summer, the company announced that it would start blocking ad blocking *on its desktop website*.

"Ads are a part of the Facebook experience; they're not a tack-on," Andrew "Boz" Bosworth, vice president of the company's ads and business platform, told *The Wall Street Journal*. Nevertheless, the Facebook guy admitted forcing people to watch ads "could irritate" them.

Did it matter? This was all being discussed in the context of desktop, which was sort of like discussing the merits of a candle next to a lightbulb. After all, Facebook made 84 percent of its vast profit from mobile advertising, per *Adweek,* which the company would *not* be blocking.

But then, just a mere two days later, the evil geniuses at AdBlock Plus announced they'd hacked Facebook's blocker of their blocker! "This is a cat-and-mouse game," said their bemused spokesman, from an undisclosed location. It seemed this to-block-or-not-to-block battle would go on and on, the textbook definition of a zero-sum game.

Later that fall, Facebook was hit by a widely reported scandal in which the company admitted it had exaggerated the time users spent watching video on the platform, video being code for "ads." But nothing much changed. For the foreseeable future, Facebook, given its enormous size and muscle, would still make the rules.

There had to be another way, a new Big Idea.

Or perhaps being better could be the big idea?

The Natives Are Restless

We call it "underwriting" because it's classier that way.

—Ira Glass, host and producer, *This American Life*

Was there *any* way traditional advertising could survive? Surely there were solutions, pleaded many Madison Avenue veterans and industry prognosticators, as they continued to perpetuate the problem. In other circles, some agencies and clients were scrambling, tossing wet tissue at the ceiling to see what might stick. There had to be some way we could be less annoying.

One fashionable response to all this chaos and uncertainty has been the rise of so-called native advertising. Unfortunately, almost no one understands what "native" actually is. So please allow me a moment to explain.

The concept of "native advertising" directly addresses the question of where an ad actually belongs. It's about context as much as content, and given all the clutter out there, we know context matters more than ever. Let's use a cheesy metaphor to drive home the point: If you are a native of Arizona, you feel a sense of belonging in Arizona. This may of course change at some point in your life. But when you connect with the place you come from, you are a native. This is not a complicated concept. We are where we hail from.

Can an ad have a sense of belonging? Do ads belong anywhere? Thanks to ad blocking, the question of belonging has become a mission-critical litmus test. Do some spaces feel like more natural places for certain ads?

Of course they do.

For instance, when you see an ad for a lipstick in the pages of *Vogue,* it's hard to disagree that such an ad seems *native* to that environment. It's difficult to fathom anyone's being annoyed by a shampoo ad next to a picture of a supermodel (unless the ad is really ugly or insultingly stupid, which isn't uncommon). However, if you should come across a television commercial for women's clothing featuring an elegant ballerina, and that ad happens to be airing in the middle of a hockey game, you might question whether that ad placement felt *native,* whether it in fact belonged there.

This is the premise behind the idea of native advertising.

In practice, making native advertising is much more complicated. What native is actually about, from the point of view of the advertising industry, concerns a far more subtle practice. It's about the *sellers* of space and audience—newspapers, magazines, podcasters, and TV networks, among others—making the ads themselves. Based on a seller's more intimate understanding of its own audience, it's about making (theoretically) more thoughtful and contextually relevant ads, rather than passively relying on someone with a less sensitive soul to place an ad in their beloved backyard.

To work the metaphor into the ground, think of it this way: Native is about brewing your own craft beer and serving it at your own soirée rather than counting on some uninvited party crasher to bring the cheap stuff.

If only it were that easy. Unsurprisingly, the rise of native advertising, and the resulting wave of experimentation it has unleashed, has caused all manner of tedious handwringing and hyperventilating that misses the forest for the trees.

If news organizations, for instance, were to start producing their own advertising for clients—and many are already doing it—did this really mean that readers would no longer be able to tell the difference between what was an ad and what was editorial? If a wildly popular podcaster like *WTF*'s Mark Maron can do a live read, switching, occasionally midsentence, between an opinion and a paid endorsement and back again, would listeners lose their minds, or at least their respect, and tune out?

And was this even a slightly new idea? This very approach—incorporating an ad into the fabric of a program rather than interrupting it—seemed permissible if the source was credible, the proof being that respected journalists such as *Slate*'s Jacob Weisberg and David Plotz were reading underwear and razor copy in the middle of their own political news podcasts, as was former Obama speechwriter Jon Favreau.

And if a publication's editorial staff had some involvement in helping brands tell their stories better, well, would that truly mark the death of journalism, and by extension the death of Western civilization? Wouldn't it just be a matter of time before all editorial independence went flying out the window if this native thing really caught on, especially when it came to covering the news? Guardians of the orthodoxy were lighting their hair on fire in protest.

To which I say . . . *Please.*

And was this really a new problem, anyway? Or was it a very old one, which felt fresh only because a new generation had failed to do its homework?

One unlikely critic of the native advertising movement is HBO's acerbic John Oliver, who enjoyed an extremely funny and ultimately misguided viral hit in 2014 when he attacked the subject, logging 7.5 million views on a matter many thought to be quite arcane. I love Oliver, but, sorry, as a noncombatant he's disqualified as a critic in this debate. As he acknowledges himself, he works for HBO, *whose business model does not require ads.*

The former *New York Times* editorial columnist Joe Nocera piled on shortly after the HBO rant went viral, penning a column in which he labeled native advertising a "slippery slope," echoing Oliver's position. Nocera cited another journalist from the nonprofit (!) Poynter Institute, who worried that the native model ran the risk of lowering the bar so low that the next step was for publishers to "ask the journalists to write the copy." Horrors.

Or perhaps not. It turns out we've seen this movie before. By way of proof, I cite our old friend, the dead advertising legend David Ogilvy, the proto Mad Man, who had the temerity to suggest that all commercials be replaced with paid TV *back in the 1960s,* thus envisioning HBO before it was invented. Ogilvy anticipated similar concerns about church being influenced by state in the following ad he wrote years ago for *Reader's Digest.* To wit:

> Ten years ago, *Reader's Digest* first opened its columns to advertising. This worried me. I was afraid that *Digest* editors would start pulling their punches in deference to advertisers—an obvious temptation to magazine editors. But this has not happened. The *Digest* has remained incorruptible.

It's so nice to hear that the *Digest* remained incorruptible! Sadly, that doesn't matter much because the

Digest is now so achingly irrelevant, it might just as well be out of business. The fact that it is actually still alive may come as a shock to some.

So let me be very clear, because this is important stuff: The purpose of native advertising is *not* to trick readers by making fake editorial out of ads, or, God forbid, to turn journalists into copywriters. It exists because the advertising industry is *obligated* to experiment with new models. If it doesn't, there is a very real chance that the entire enterprise will face an extinction event.

John Oliver doesn't have to worry about that. Again, thanks to HBO, he's not reliant on ads. He's one of the lucky ones. The *Times*'s Nocera and his ilk should worry more about the nontrivial possibility that publishers will slowly run out of ad revenue as traditional advertising goes away and subscription revenue cannot make up for the loss. If that outcome comes to pass, he will no longer have to fret about the meaning of "native" advertising because the Gray Lady will be six feet under. Which won't happen, by the way, because the people actually running the show there are very, very smart.

What's Old Is New Again

As you may have noticed, I like daring Adland to experiment with new creative models. I also encourage it to take a fresh look at *old* advertising models. In fact, from where I sit, it appears that many of the older forms of advertising, the really old ones, the older the better, make the most sense in our modern media world.

Take, for instance, the idea of brand sponsorship and brand integration. One need only cite programs like *Kraft Mystery Theatre* or *Mutual of Omaha's Wild Kingdom,* and a hundred other examples dating back to Procter & Gamble's invention of the soap opera, to know that there was once a great tradition of brands underwriting programming, a far gentler and kinder form of advertising, as PBS has known for years, than sticking one's thumb into someone else's pie.

Of course, the idea of a brand underwriting a program takes many forms—from pure white-glove sponsorship, to product placement, to content directly produced by the brand, which might be called brand storytelling.

At its core, this approach is usually rooted in the sincere insight that any of those options is better than making ads that people *hate.* The elegant integration of a brand into a program—think most recently of the role of Avion tequila in *Entourage*—is always a bit trickier, but the approach, especially when it works, should be applauded.

Unsurprisingly, this model also has its critics. The people doing the critiquing seem to have overlooked the roiling market dynamics in play and instead adopted the role of defenders of the faith. Take *The New Yorker's*

Ken Auletta and Emily Nussbaum. Auletta recently asked a prominent Google executive at a private event whether native advertising "was in the public interest." I would counter by asking whether traditional advertising is in the public interest. Meanwhile, Nussbaum, in a recent column, reflexively assumed the worst about the motive behind brands attempting to navigate their way out of a dying model, thus completely missing the larger point: that good ads are better than bad ads, for everyone.

Instead Nussbaum assumes that the attempt to make more creative brand-driven content is a plot: "It's a sedative designed to make viewers feel that there's nothing to be angry about," she writes of attempts at brand integration. Actually, I would argue that a lot more consumers are angry about annoying traditional commercial interruptions. Fortunately, as if sensing how naive her point of view is, Nussbaum caveats her point: "Perhaps this makes me sound like a drunken twenty-two-year-old waving a battered copy of Naomi Klein's *No Logo*."

Yes, it does, Emily. But no matter. For now, you still have *The New Yorker*. But unless Eustace Tilly can survive in a world without ads, which he may well have to, we'll need to be more open to alternate ways of getting you paid. Me, I'm more worried about the *sober* twenty-two-year-olds, the ones who won't look at a traditional ad, ever, under any circumstances. And about the challenges this presents to the people who have logos to sell. Ironically, it's an old challenge, as evidenced by the nineteenth-century mission statement of the *Vermont Caledonian,* a long-since-closed newspaper:

> Here shall the press
> The people's rights maintain,
> Unawed by influence
> And unbribed by gain.

While the *New Yorker* critics were caviling against new ad models and indirectly defending a broken and much-despised status quo, Vice, the media company most gifted at using a putative fluency with the folkways of millennials, was finally getting its own TV station. As of November 2015, Vice would be taking over H2, a little-watched channel on A&E, one of Vice's parent companies, and rebooting it as Viceland. Though it was in its early days, there was much media coverage around a statement from gray-bearded Vice CEO Shane Smith indicating that Viceland would reinvent the increasingly unwelcome concept of traditional advertising. "We will test new and innovative monetization strategies," Smith said, "placing Viceland at the pointy tip of the spear of the rapidly changing terrain of TV advertising." Dude!

No one knew exactly what this pointy tip was, or if it would pass muster with the likes of Nussbaum. But it was clear that it wouldn't mean "spots and dots," aka traditional thirty-second TV spots and Web banner ads. Because for any new media company truly in tune with young eyeballs, those were no longer viable.

A new normal would be necessary. The old box wasn't working anymore, and everyone would have to think outside it.

All Over but the Shouting

So let's recap.

At the risk of being redundant, I'm here to argue that advertising as we know it—except on live sports and the social media platform of the moment, give or take—is *over*. I come not to praise it, in case you hadn't noticed, but to bury it.

I believe the only miracle cure for this terminal patient, the only ray of hope for advertising's survival, is creativity.

I believe that this is excellent news, both for civilians and advertisers. And it's why I have a burning urge to engage in mouth-to-mouth resuscitation.

This seems like a good time to revisit my bona fides.

As I mentioned earlier, I spent a decade on the front lines of the ad business as CEO for what is generally considered to be the world's greatest creative agency, Droga5, an agency known for compelling storytelling, the best work in the business. I had a great run, but from my unique promontory atop the highest highs of a chronically lowbrow industry, untouched by its worst impulses, I observed that nothing had really changed, and things in fact were getting worse for the rest of the industry, that it was crumbling and that the consequences of this pending collapse were not yet fully clear. One could be actively disrupting the dowagers of Madison Avenue and still find those best intentions drowned by the suction of a sinking ship.

So at the risk of stating the obvious, this isn't a eulogy. No one should cry at advertising's funeral, especially me.

But this isn't an obituary, but rather a memento mori. For here's the bittersweet part: As traditional advertising goes away, people will still need to buy and sell things; we'll still need to know what's new. It would be wise to learn from the mistakes of the past rather than repeat them.

The question for tomorrow will be not what, but *how* brands communicate, especially when the fundamental rules of engagement no longer apply. Unlike many naysayers, I'm actually optimistic about what will take the place of traditional advertising, about the brave new landscape that lies ahead.

On the other hand, I'm brutally realistic about entropy, and how hard it will be to bring this dying industry back from the brink. I'd like to believe that what you hold in your hands might provide some with a road map for the future, a prediction of what the world could look like when advertising, as it was once understood, finally ceases to exist.

Except, of course, for the Super Bowl . . .

Among the more pleasing by-products of the coming end of advertising is a heretical realization among some industry thinkers: the idea that for advertising to survive, or rather to thrive, *it must add value to people's lives*. In a world in which lazy, superfluous, and stupid no longer cut it, advertising will have no choice but to compete as primary content, not secondary intrusion. It will become the thing, not the thing that sells the thing.

Such a value exchange comes in many shapes and sizes, but it can entail everything from simply trying harder to not be annoying, à la Larry Page, to providing utility, services, gifts, joint ventures, investment, and even patronage of the arts. In some instances, simply shutting up could be the best strategy, as when a brand underwrites quality programming, commercial-free, an act of inspired generosity and kindness.

There's an old adage in the ad business that "telling isn't selling." Yes, the purpose of advertising is to sell things, and no one should think otherwise, but there's no longer any credible reason why that mission must be synonymous with insulting people's intelligence, or must take the form of shouting at them or forcing them to watch something they hate. Smart marketers are increasingly embracing the idea that they can no longer just say, they must *do*. They must consider a higher purpose, and even dabble in metaphysics.

Or like Lego, the eighty-three-year-old Danish company, they can make a hit movie about themselves, garner an Academy Award nomination, and take home nearly $500 million, according to *Variety,* from the global box office. Proof that the concept of "branded" entertainment, when done properly, is remarkably effective. Or as Lego's Michael McNally told *Adweek,* "We would rather people need us than try to make people want us."

This isn't just pure whimsy or the sour grapes of a recovering ad executive. Beyond *The Lego Movie,* there are many examples out there of legitimate options that exist beyond traditional advertising, many of which will be discussed in depth later in this book. I'll prove it, I hope, by citing what is perhaps the most successful demonstration of this ambitious new advertising model: Citi Bike.

It should be clear to anyone that the New York City bike-share program Citi Bike (which I had nothing to do with) is *advertising,* though certainly not advertising in any way it is commonly understood. In case you missed it, the program is spelled Citi, not City, and the blue paint on every one of those six thousand bicycles now brightening New York is the bank's signature gradient of Pantone 286C.

So, yes, those Citi Bikes are an "ad" for the parent company. That said, that same parent coughed up a budget of $41 million, per Citibank's own reporting, and rather than squandering that eight-figure investment on useless pollution, they built something additive that actually reduces our carbon footprint. When a corporate behemoth expands its communication strategy from traditional commercials (which, in all fairness, Citibank still makes) to providing bikes for six thousand New Yorkers to pedal across the Brooklyn Bridge, the time-space continuum has changed forever.

Many will grouse that this is a small price to pay for Citibank's role in the financial crisis, and that's a valid point. But it's better than what used to be, and far more useful than the passive sponsorship of a baseball stadium, another retrograde form of advertising. What we have here is the creation of an entirely new channel, one that serves a function rather than needlessly interrupting an existing one.

I applaud Citi Bike for its vision, and for demonstrating how marketing can change the world. It couldn't have been easy to push such a program up what was surely a Sisyphean mountain of bureaucracy and orthodoxy.

Wouldn't it be interesting to see more advertisers follow suit and create new paths rather than befoul existing ones? One example might be targeting our aging infrastructure, our blighted bridges and highways, as a media channel. After all, it's perhaps the last place where human beings are still receptive to advertising, and the timing couldn't be better: City and state governments are broke.

And the advertising industry still has a cool trillion, give or take a few hundred million, to spend on more appreciated forms. Use it or lose it.

The serendipitous confluence of municipal poverty and secular change in marketing practices presents a unique opportunity for a new breed of public-private partnerships. For instance, why not have Verizon pay to refurbish our dilapidated subways in exchange for its logo on a line? Perhaps that might have been a better marketing investment than the widely reported $4.8 billion it paid for Yahoo.

What if Pfizer took a chunk of the money it spends on unpleasant direct-to-consumer advertising (please, no more warnings about four-hour erections), and fixed the Brooklyn-Queens Expressway instead? The opportunities are limitless. Besides, we've already got bad advertising on the subway; we already allow mom-and-pop sponsorship of our highways. Let's do it properly and celebrate the companies that might step up to pay for it. They need new places to put their messages, and we need fewer potholes.

This is the new Big Idea: Brands can make the world a better place, and they can sell more merchandise doing it.

Advertising as we know it is not the answer. Imagination, creativity, and an active distaste for pollution are the new necessary ingredients, along with the ability to see the difference between authenticity and artifice. And, of course, dollars, which brands have in droves. It just requires a reallocation of resources, and talent with the vision, character, and courage to implement those resources appropriately.

As I said before, one of the most inspiring sayings in the advertising business is "Brand love equals brand dollars." Sometimes it's actually true. I've always been struck by the cultish intensity with which people worship the brands they love—from Audi to Hermès to Warby Parker—and the visceral hatred they feel for most advertising. But now this dichotomy is finally blurring, and what George Orwell famously called "the rattling of a stick inside a swill pail" will soon be silenced.

It was Orwell, of course, whose infamous *1984* inspired one of the best television commercials of all time, Apple's epic Macintosh Super Bowl launch spot. What is often forgotten about that spot is that it aired only once.

But not to worry: You can still find it on YouTube, if you don't mind putting up with the pre-roll.

Part Two

Advertising's Origins

Floating Soap, Snake Oil, and Smack

Many a small thing has been made large by the right kind of advertising.

—Mark Twain, *A Connecticut Yankee in King Arthur's Court,* 1889

Did you make us—or did we make you?

—XTC, "Dear God," 1986

In the old world, you devoted 30 percent of your time to building a great service and 70 percent of your time to shouting about it. In the new world, that inverts.

—Jeff Bezos's Top Ten Leadership Lessons

O f the many self-congratulatory chestnuts coughed up by Madison Avenue over the years, *"Nothing kills a bad product faster than good advertising"* may be the most laughable.

The idea, coined by industry legend Bill Bernbach, one of the founders of DDB, the creative agency best known for its legendary 1959 campaign for the Volkswagen Beetle (THINK SMALL), argues that a great ad draws unwanted attention to a terrible item that might otherwise have escaped consumer dissatisfaction.

If only that were true.

Sadly, the line gives the advertising industry too much credit. For starters, as evidenced by the explosive rise of ad blocking, the bad product has often been advertising itself. And then there's the unfortunate fact that the ad business grew to such an enormous size, in many cases, thanks to its unrivaled wizardry for elevating bad products.

It's almost impossible to imagine today, when bad products—from lame resorts to awful movies—get crucified on user-generated forums like Yelp and Rotten Tomatoes no matter how much money they squander on marketing. But in advertising's early days, it was hard to know what was a good product and what wasn't. In fact, what seemed to be a great product often turned out to be very, very bad indeed. Just ask the people who created the Marlboro Man. On the other hand, certain products that seemed trivial were made indispensable once advertising created a desire for them. Like chewing gum or Lemon Pledge.

Yes, the great-ad/bad-product/bad-ad/great-product debate perfectly encapsulates advertising's fatal flaw: the tension between authenticity and artifice. Two centuries after the birth of the modern construct we've come to know as Madison Avenue, those contrary forces still continue their complicated interdependency. But this compound has grown increasingly unsustainable, and its long-overdue unraveling is yet another reason advertising is headed for extinction.

So does good advertising kill a bad product? Does a good product need advertising? Did bad products kill advertising? Or did it turn out that bad advertising was the failed product that ultimately killed advertising?

To unwrap this riddle, we must go back to where it all began.

For in advertising's origins, we can chronicle its death foretold.

Nothing Sells like Soap: The Pure Lure of Authentic Ads

Sometime in the early days of 1837, smack in the middle of one of America's more bruising if less infamous financial crises, two decades before the first musket fire of the Civil War, a pair of industrious and earnest immigrants named William Procter and James Gamble set up a humble soap- and candle-making incubator on the muddy banks of the Cincinnati River.

These guys may never inspire their own *Hamilton,* but their story is as inherently all-American as any immigrant tale. Procter was English. He made candles and ran the company store. Gamble, who was Irish, made the soap. They both had a vision for a better world elevated by their quality products. Both had excellent hair. They were frequently depicted scowling with intense sincerity. Today, they'd be artisanal chocolate makers in Williamsburg or brogrammers in Palo Alto, right down to Procter's hipster beard-without-a-mustache look.

They were family, too, brothers-in-law actually, conjoined by wives who happened to be sisters. The boys really hadn't planned on partnering, but the grueling recession of '37 persuaded them to join forces (with a little urging from their father-in-law). And so, somewhat reluctantly, they set up shop, bootstrapped with $7,192.24 of the old man's capital, about $175K in 2016 dollars.

The business chugged along nicely if unspectacularly for a few decades. Then a serendipitous discovery produced their historic contribution to our national narrative: Ivory Soap.

Soon after Ivory Soap came the ads for Ivory Soap. And once Procter & Gamble started advertising, it literally never stopped. The company would go on to make every sort of ad imaginable and invent unprecedented formats. Though other young companies of the era helped shape the ad business as we know it, it's fair to say that without P&G, many of the very concepts we associate today with traditional advertising might not exist.

One hundred fifty years later, by the start of the twenty-first century, P&G had blossomed into a $40 billion global giant, according to *Bloomberg Businessweek*, home to some of the biggest, most brilliantly marketed brands on the planet, all built on the back of a single bar of very important soap.

• • •

But why did it all begin with Ivory?

What was so special about a single bar of suds?

The simple answer is that America, circa the mid-nineteenth century, needed a shower. We had a genuine need to wash, though many of us didn't know it.

Around the time that Ivory Soap arrived, America was a smelly, filthy, uncultured land, mostly rural and agricultural in nature. "Large numbers were more or less illiterate, had little money and were quite credulous," says the Madison Avenue scholar Roland Marchand in *Advertising the American Dream: Making Way for Modernity*. That blissful guilelessness meant that few had any idea that stinky body odor could be an issue, let alone a liability. Few also cared back then about brands, or at least certain kinds of brands. Soap, for the most part, was a commodity.

That all changed on a dreary spring morning in 1870, when a P&G employee found that using vegetable oil in its generic soap formula instead of tallow or lard would make it float. It might sound unremarkable today, but this was an innovation up there with popping corn or one-hundred-forty-character communication. Moreover, this new lightweight iteration was cheaper to manufacture than olive oil soap and yet still felt premium.

The company could have called it "Procter & Gamble's White Soap"—such humdrum labels were the way most honest products told their story back then—but

Harley Procter, the cofounder's ambitious son, knew something catchier was required to cut through and create a sense of . . . *covetousness.*

It turns out young Harley had his famous marketing epiphany in church, proving that God truly does move in mysterious ways. Harley was musing on how to sell his new soap when he heard the following psalm: *"All thy garments smell of myrrh and aloes and cassia out of the ivory palaces whereby they have made thee glad."* According to *Rising Tide,* the official biography of P&G, Harley said, *"There, that is the name!"* He took out a handkerchief and scribbled down a rudimentary logo and package design; the name was trademarked shortly thereafter. The first Ivory Soap ad would soon appear in *Grocers' Criterion.*

Like "The Facebook," it was originally called "The Ivory."

P&G's timing was impeccable. At the start of the 1880s, the consumer packaged goods business was getting extremely crowded. Joseph Campbell was ramping up the canned soup trade. Henry J. Heinz was bottling condiments like ketchup. John and William Kellogg were reinventing breakfast. William Wrigley, who also started in the soap trade, had pivoted to chewing gum. All these rivals were looking for a way to differentiate themselves. Good advertising could tell the tale.

So P&G aggressively embraced what T. J. Jackson Lears, author of *Fables of Abundance: A Cultural History of Advertising in America,* called "a patina of sincerity, science and progress." Or, to put it another way, they proved that nothing could accelerate the success of a great product like spending lots of money on great advertising.

Quality advertising, P&G promised, would become "a permanent part of the policy of The Procter & Gamble Co." A memo from the period proclaimed that making ads was not "a 'flash in the pan' proposition intended to impress the dealer and get him to 'load up.'" No, this company was going to support its genuine commitment to product with sincere communications.

One early Ivory ad nicely encapsulates this evangelical belief in authenticity:

> Ivory Soap came like a ray of light across our
>   darkened way
> And now we're civil, kind and good
> And keep the laws as people should . . .

It may not be music to today's ear, but one could see a nineteenth-century shopper swooning.

As the company leaned further into tugging heartstrings to accentuate its product, Ivory would simplify its claim and boil its message down to a single emotion-infused reason to believe: IVORY SOAP. IT FLOATS, a motto that would be advertised ad infinitum and resonate widely—and be emulated for years by players from Apple to Nike.

Thanks to P&G's focus, which came with a meaningful financial investment, the nascent ad business took notice. The ambitious men starting to populate the ad trade in the East turned their attention to the Midwest. Word spread. Out in Cincinnati there was a deep-pocketed client whose products didn't trouble one's conscience, like some of the lesser products many ad men had taken to selling, which we will get to in a moment.

New advertising firms sprang up to service the likes of P&G and other legitimate packaged goods companies. These new agencies were made up of white-shoed WASPs, educated at elite Northeastern schools. There was N. W. Ayer, who would start the first major full-service advertising firm in America, and J. Walter Thompson (who started at $15 a week in 1902), soon to be the richest ad man in New York City, not to mention such players as Young & Rubicam, Leo Burnett, Ogilvy & Mather, BBDO, DDB, McCann, and Grey. Incredibly, all these firms are still around today, a testament to America's insatiable appetites.

Suddenly, the advertising industry was producing work so welcome that people actually collected it, a concept hard to fathom in this age of widespread ad blocking. In many homes, early "chromolithographic" ads torn out of magazines became the closest thing the average American family came to owning art, "the chief means of brightening a dreary visual environment," according to Lears. As the journalist Samuel Hopkins Adams wrote in 1909, "Think how much duller your ride to business would be if the car hoardings were blank, instead of being filled with color and print. They are decent and companionable myths, these folk of Ad-Land."

Many at these new ad firms worked hard to make a contribution to society. How could one add value while still driving consumption? At some point, it became fashionable to hire genuine artists to make ads: The painter Maxfield Parrish did a Jell-O ad and made a poster about colanders for GE; the photographer Edward Steichen worked on contract for Ayer and J. Walter Thompson. JWT approached Margaret Bourke-White to shoot on contract and make its work "less artificial." George Bernard Shaw and H. G. Wells toiled for Harrods in London. Georgia O'Keeffe did a Dole Pineapple campaign.

Meanwhile, young Harley Procter was putting his money where his mouth was. He craved as many canvases as possible on which to herald his message. Procter went on a spending tear, doubling and soon tripling Ivory Soap's budget and running full-page ads in such newspapers and magazines as *Ladies' Home Journal, The*

Saturday Evening Post, Harper's, and *Scribner's.* In doing so, he and his kin parented the fledgling mass print industry, flooding early newspapers and magazines with a lucrative rain of ad dollars and helping to scale and secure the adjacency model that would later inform, and then ruin, Internet advertising.

Nothing Sells like Snake Oil: The Magical Power of Artifice

The age of Ivory was a heady time in Adland. Early execs, especially the ad men who worked at those white-shoe firms, were likely excited by the opportunity to tell the story of P&G products and others like them. It was honorable work, true storytelling, and the skill was in the story well told. And they were the good guys.

After all, there was already another class of products out there, a lesser category where many of their colleagues plied their trade. Those products were all about patina, not sincerity.

Long before the invention of Ivory Soap, the advertising of American consumer packaged goods had become a choice between artifice and authenticity. There were legitimate products such as Ivory, Wrigley's gum, and Campbell's soup. And then there was snake oil: scams, miracle cures, and other frauds, a vast sea of unregulated, often dangerous products that, unlike the famous ad man mantra, all succeeded via great advertising.

All of this meant that the rapidly expanding ad industry endured a constant tension between "aspirations for respectability and their disreputable clientele," according to Lears. Sure, it was more appealing to be an honest craftsman than a bunco artist, but who made a better living? In truth, both types of advertising paid very well, though the scam artists were likely paid more. This choice came to be known as "trash for cash."

But what sort of trash are we talking about, anyway? What bad product could make an ad man blush? And why was it so easy to shill?

In mid-nineteenth-century America, soap wasn't the only product people needed. Getting clean was appealing, but lots of people were in flat-out pain. America may have been widely unwashed, but most of us were probably too uncomfortable to care. For many, there was the far more urgent need to be cured. Or to just feel a little less bad.

Back then, we were a nation suffering from constant aches and pains, perpetually gassy, gouty, and constipated. And then there were the more threatening ailments, such as tuberculosis. People were hungry for anything that might help.

Toward this demand rushed a new supply conceived to take advantage of our national discomfort and anxiety: an expansive array of fake medicines that were more about boastful claims and sensational labels than efficacy.

Ads didn't kill these bad products, as the saying goes, they fueled them. To this day, that gift for slinging snake oil, for selling something that probably shouldn't be sold, remains part of advertising's unique heritage, and why it's often reflexively despised.

For the entire second half of the nineteenth century, the nascent American pharmacy was overrun with a panoply of quack remedies and so-called patent medicines, rogue products endowed with wonderfully silly, over-the-top names such as "Mrs. Winslow's Soothing Syrup" and "Hooper's Anodyne, the Infant's Friend," both of which were generously laced with opium (and blithely given to children). Nice.

Thinking about it today makes your average CVS seem especially boring. Back then, drugstore shelves were flush with widely advertised swill like Hostetter's Stomach Bitters and Peruna, both made with 43.3 percent alcohol. Products like Merchant's Gargling Oil, Upham's Freckle, Tan and Pimple Banisher, Sanford's Liver Invigorator, Fetridge's Balm of a Thousand Flowers, Laird's Bloom of Youth, and Fellows' Hypophosphites are just a sampling of the many fanciful nostrums that fought for space at the neighborhood apothecary and stuffed newspapers and magazines with ads. No modern midcentury home was complete without three or four bottles of this rubbish in the medicine cabinet. No paper could be read without seeing pages and pages of advertisements for such products.

Yes, snake oil was a big business. So making ads for snake oil rapidly became a big business, too. During this gilded and utterly unregulated age, the makers of these remedies—again, many of them just cleverly packaged opium or alcohol—quickly became the first big-spending clients for the emerging world of professional advertising, rivaling or paying more than P&G and its colleagues. Some agencies refused to work with them, but most of them did.

Drug manufacturers, according to Marchand, were extremely savvy advertisers. For instance, they were the first American businessmen "to recognize the power of the catchphrase, the identifiable logo and trademark, the celebrity endorsement, the appeal to social success." The word "brand" wasn't used back then, at least in its current form, but this is where it all began.

As with any disproportionately powerful client, the snake oil industry pushed the envelope on the nascent ad industry's codes and ethics. When it came to the manner in which these remedies were marketed, there were no rules. It was the Wild West; anything that worked was welcome. And what worked most was to be loud and lurid. Whatever one could think up to say was worth saying.

Once just a step up from common peddlers, ad men became poets of pep, imaginative storytellers crafting myths about attributes that were entirely nonexistent. Patent medicine advertisements were "shamefully and flagrantly disreputable in their fake selling claims," according to Lears. The early ad man "fused with carnival barkers and such promoters of ballyhoo and humbug as P. T. Barnum."

Not only did these early unethical ad men learn to excel at crafting bold lies, they invented such time-tested concepts as the paid testimonial and selling directly to doctors. Individual MDs were targeted and taught—just as they are today by modern pharmaceutical companies—how to directly prescribe to patients.

Doctors and pharmacists had no choice but to improve their professional standing or be implicated in all that hokum and horseshit. Thus were born the American Medical Association and the American Pharmaceutical Association. Having organized, these trade unions demanded that big-budget campaigns shilling dubious treatments to the public be stopped. Or at least be subject to scrutiny or stricter regulation.

But that would take a while. And for some time, there was no stopping the snake oil syndicate. Following a boom in Lower Manhattan, on Park Row (Madison Avenue wouldn't be the industry epicenter until 1923), agencies sprang up in Philadelphia, Boston, and Chicago. The skill most in demand was a gift for charm, yarn spinning, and salesmanship. Mark Twain nicely illustrates the character of the contemporary bunco artist in his 1873 satiric novel, *The Gilded Age:* "The colonel's tongue was a magician's wand that turned dried apples into figs and water into wine as easily as one could change a hovel into a palace and present poverty into future riches."

Meanwhile, President William Howard Taft, a man of few words, decried the industry's "evil tendencies." And yet patent medicine marketing became ever more pervasive.

Nothing quite captures the tone and spirit of the time better than one of the first known ads for Coca-Cola, which of course was originally promoted as a remedy:

> To the invigorating properties of the Coca leaf are added the sustain [*sic*] properties of the Cola Nut. Relieves fatigue that comes from over-working or over-thinking. Puts vim and "go" into tired brains and weary bodies.

Coke was also marketed as "a valuable Brain Tonic and cure for all nerve affections [*sic*]." This, of course, was before 1903, when the company removed the notorious active ingredient that fueled all that "vim and go."

By 1906, things were starting to change as people began to wise up. That year, the United States passed its first piece of legislation on the matter, the Pure Food and Drug Act. Much of this was in response to the muckraking work of the great American journalist Samuel Hopkins Adams, who did an entire series on "the nostrum evil" for the magazine *Collier's Weekly*.

Having studied the remedy business, Adams concluded, "Fraud, exploited by the skillfullest [*sic*] of advertising bunco men, is the basis of the trade." Incensed, Adams sought to end the harm done to the public by "tyrannical masters," men whose sole purpose was "the parting of a fool and his money." According to T. J. Jackson Lears, the bunco artist had turned advertising into "a stench in the nostrils of the civilized world."

More than a hundred years later, we no longer have patent remedies on the pharmacy shelf, at least not in such crude form. But that stench can sometimes still be detected today. And perhaps that's why so many find advertising so annoying. People can tolerate only so much bullshit.

Imagine what ad blockers could have done to Fetridge's Balm of a Thousand Flowers.

Nothing Scores like Smack: When a Bad Product Turns Out to Be Really Bad, Despite the Great Advertising

Sometime in the fall of 2016, Bayer, the German chemical colossus, made a blockbuster offer of $56 billion to acquire Monsanto, the U.S. seed giant, according to Reuters. The vision was to create the world's largest pharmaceutical and pesticide conglomerate. (Now there are two words you rarely see in the same sentence.)

I know you can read. Nevertheless, the size of the potential transaction bears repeating: *fifty-plus billion.* With a *b.* That's a lot of Aspirin.

A lot of Aspirin indeed, and more power to Bayer. Because Bayer invented this miracle drug more than a hundred years ago, and it's still going strong today. Bayer deserves all the profit it can reap from that astonishing act of ingenuity, and for the decades of brilliant marketing that made Aspirin so popular.

And Bayer is entitled to feel proud, too, for despite a vast portfolio of other products, Bayer's entire corporate identity is wrapped in that iconic brand, in its purity and unrivaled elegant effectiveness.

Yes, Aspirin is very much a *brand,* a fiercely defended one. It's not a generic substance, just as Ivory could never be simply a soap, which is why I elect to capitalize it. Whether or not Bayer clears the steep hurdles required to close such an enormous deal—it was unclear at press time—the value of the company is the ultimate testament to Aspirin's remarkable success. #Respect.

The success of Aspirin also represents an incredibly instructive story about the nature of advertising, and another example of the industry's complicated relationship with authenticity and artifice—and the rare occasion when what seems to be authentic turns out to be artificial.

Because the story of Aspirin's success also includes the remarkable failure of one of the most shrewdly advertised bad products of all time, Aspirin's little-known black sheep twin brother.

They say nothing kills a bad product faster than good advertising. We've seen that this is rarely the case. What follows is the rare example when it's actually true.

About twenty-five years after P&G was conceived along the Cincinnati River in Ohio, Bayer came into being on the eastern bank of the Rhine, in the tiny industrial town of Leverkusen, Germany. It, too, was the work of men with smartly cultivated facial hair, of the sort now found on tattooed mixologists brewing absinthe varietals in subterranean cocktail lounges.

If Ivory is the most popular soap ever made, it's fair to

say that Aspirin, which Bayer invented in the summer of 1898, is the most successful drug of all time, a medicine beloved by moms across the planet, a product synonymous with anodyne but unfailingly reliable pain relief, a harmless and simple medicine whose magical properties extend from relieving basic aches and pains to supporting cardiovascular health.

In many ways, Aspirin was the pill that single-handedly killed the snake oil industry. No artifice, no matter how well advertised, could stand up to Aspirin's turn-of-the-century, state-of-the-art, German-lab-crafted authenticity.

But Aspirin was far from an overnight success. At the time of its launch, the drug not only had to compete with the din of relentless patent medicine advertising, it was also competing with another new drug launched by Bayer, a drug that was essentially Aspirin's twin brother.

This drug had been invented a mere two weeks earlier, by the same three young scientists who invented Aspirin. And this drug, which showed tremendous promise, would be more of a corporate priority for Bayer than Aspirin.

The name of this new drug, a powerful synthesis of the active ingredient in opium, was Heroin.

This is a true story, by the way.

• • •

Heroin made its 1898 debut at the annual gathering of the Congress of German Naturalists and Physicians, a tweedy convocation of some fifteen hundred academics. An exec at Bayer presented it as a synthetic cough medicine ten times more effective than the current folk remedies of choice.

Two months later, Heroin officially shipped to nearly universal acclaim—and seemingly unlimited commercial potential, driven by intensive advertising. Within a single year, Bayer had produced nearly a ton of the stuff, selling it in twenty-three countries. Meanwhile, Aspirin was shelved *for eighteen months.*

By 1900, Heroin dwarfed all the other brands in Bayer's portfolio. It proved to be especially popular in America. "It was a big mistake to make it so cheap," one of its creators complained at a Bayer marketing meeting.

By the start of the twentieth century, Heroin was sold in pastilles, lozenges, and salts. Unlike untrustworthy remedies such as Mrs. Winslow's Soothing Syrup and Hooper's Anodyne, "the Infant's Friend," which would soon be exposed for encouraging Americans to administer opium to their children, Heroin was considered extremely respectable. Much of this respectability was the result of its sober advertising. Indeed, one might call it a patina of sincerity, science, and progress, very much the same tone of authenticity perfected by the good people at P&G.

To further expand the Heroin trade, Bayer began targeting physicians, an unsavory practice that still goes on today, sometimes for compensation. A common early ad refrain: "Order a supply from your jobber!" Hundreds of favorable clinical papers on Heroin were soon published around the world, a form of advertising that would be reprinted in myriad newspapers and magazines. Many doctors would write testimonials, applauding the drug as a fine cough suppressant. The *Boston Medical and Surgical Journal* raved, "Heroin possesses many advantages. It's not hypnotic, and there's no danger of acquiring a habit."

Why did this technique prove so effective? Because, as P&G proved, advertising that leveraged authenticity wrapped in utility almost always works. There was no need for jazz-hands-style hyperbole. "There's no need to oversell a product that can really cure you," says the award-winning ad man David Droga, who made his reputation by avoiding such traps. "They already had what might be the world's most captive audience."

Heroin could cure, but of course it could also kill. After a decade or so, America began to increasingly interrogate its drug problem, having already questioned its susceptibility to snake oil.

At first, synthetic drugs from fancy German factories escaped scrutiny. But evidence began to pile up across the globe, as any reader could predict through the privilege of hindsight, that Heroin was in fact extremely addictive. By 1912, the Hague Opium Convention called for control of *all* narcotics, including Heroin. With the 1914 Harrison Act, the War on Drugs officially began, and Bayer's Heroin was its first casualty.

Meanwhile, by 1906, Aspirin had come to account for 25 percent of Bayer's total sales in the United States, according to Diarmuid Jeffreys's excellent *Aspirin: The Remarkable Story of a Wonder Drug.* The brand had, to borrow a phrase, gone viral. One of Bayer's singular advertising innovations was to stamp each pill with a so-called trust mark, an iconic symbol that endures to this day, the coveted point of difference to which all great brands aspire. In doing so, Bayer created the first-ever official logo for a drug, fashioning a playbook that extends today from the Nike "swoosh" to McDonald's golden arches.

These days, Bayer sells a remarkable forty billion Aspirin tablets a year, generating $4 billion in annual revenue, per its own reporting. And when it comes to the official Bayer party line, Heroin might as well have never existed at all. Any mention of the world's most notorious controlled substance has been thoroughly redacted from the company's record. Bayer simply refuses to acknowledge its role in Heroin's paternity, even in passing. If success has many fathers, then Heroin is an orphan.

Oddly, despite Bayer's lack of interest, the Heroin *brand* is thriving; the proverbial black sheep just keeps getting bigger. Which proves that advertising comes in many forms, and in many qualities, but nothing works quite like word of mouth and a strong brand name.

More than a hundred years since it was created and sold as a legitimate alternative to bad medicine, the Heroin brand is bigger and stronger than ever, a universally infamous icon whose unrivaled pain-killing properties have generated billions of dollars in illicit revenue—and millions of broken hearts and busted lives.

So who won the first battle between authenticity and artifice in the advertising industry?

By the end of World War I, legitimate products had clearly triumphed over snake oil, most of which had been regulated out of business. The practitioners of authenticity, for the most part, had the upper hand. The third way that was Heroin, once the essence of sincerity, science, and progress, endured as an illegal outlier, no longer in need of any advertising.

Meanwhile, Procter & Gamble and other packaged goods companies were dramatically increasing their advertising budgets and the ways in which they deployed them. They made newspaper and magazine ads, posters, streamers, and streetcar ads. They invented the promotional mass mailer, known to some as junk mail, and helped create the concept of direct marketing. They turned their own packaging into a channel on which to tell their story. They invested in the best data they could collect, presaging the sophisticated analytics firms of today.

"P&G changed deep-rooted habits and social customs inside a generation or two," writes Wally Olins, the corporate identity guru, in his book *On Brand,* "and transformed the lives of housewives." Alongside Heinz, Kellogg, and others, these companies "took branding out of the semi-reputable world of the medicine chest [and] into the kitchen."

Thanks to P&G, Americans washed themselves more thoroughly and more often. They also washed their clothes more frequently. They ate a more varied diet. In no small way—thanks to Ivory, Tide, Crest, Olay, Downy, Bounty, and myriad others—America can credit P&G for the fact that we live longer, smell fresher, and have better teeth.

Others have suggested that P&G's relentless advertising consigned a nation of Americans to a life of domestic servitude, lemminglike consumerism, and constant paranoia about bad breath, soiled laundry, and body odor. But that's another book . . .

There was no looking back. The company and others like it marched forward, spending more and more on their ad budgets. By the late 1920s, *The Saturday Evening Post* would feature an index of advertisers right next to its editorial table of contents. And in 1926, President Calvin Coolidge would praise the industry for "cultivation of the mind and social graces."

Radio Ga-Ga and the Thirty-Second Revolution

Things might have continued in perpetuity from there, a series of endless authentic product messages printed on a two-dimensional media landscape of magazines and newspapers, catalogs and posters, and other paper surfaces. But then a massive new disruptive technology arrived to change everything.

In an age of self-driving cars and virtual reality, it's hard to imagine what a huge game changer radio was, but rarely has a medium so quickly reinvented advertising.

Brands quickly took notice, and not surprisingly, few took notice faster than P&G. After years of essentially underwriting the newspaper and magazine business—according to Davis Dyer's *Rising Tide,* P&G's total print budget by the end of the 1920s was $3.2 million, more than a million more than its next competitor, Colgate—the company embraced radio with a vengeance.

As on any new proving ground, the industry's dignity was at stake. Despite advertising's grudging respectability, the stigma of its snake oil salesman DNA lingered about the business like so much cheap cologne. The consensus was that radio was an opportunity to apply new artistry that would further distance the industry from its tendency toward artifice. Radio demanded "more seeing, less selling," according to Lears.

The solution was a radical new idea, or rather a very old idea in new clothes: a so-called soap opera, in which a brand could produce actual content rather than make the thing adjacent to the content. *Ma Perkins,* arguably the first radio soap opera, debuted in 1933, sponsored by P&G's Oxydol brand, featuring "America's first mother on the air."

The soap opera soon became the gold standard on radio, and P&G, as it had done before in print, would soon also own the airwaves. Since the company now stewarded some two hundred brands, there was a lot to say, and a lot to sell. Unlike print, with its pesky "church and state" editorial guidelines, radio could be completely controlled by the advertiser, and nothing sold a good product like good advertising.

Radio was a godsend to the business. It "seemed to

solve the advertiser's perennial problem of introducing the product," as a JWT executive noted in 1930. With its theater of the mind, radio created a "natural, uncommercial [*sic*] atmosphere, weaving it into a seamless web of illusory 'real life.'" One might even say that on the radio, ads were inherently "native" to the format.

And as radio took off, so did American consumption. According to *Advertising, the Uneasy Persuasion,* you could find a total of nine hundred items for sale circa 1928. By 1946, there were three thousand products in the marketplace. Things could have cruised along nicely from there.

And then, just a few years later, another new technology came along to change everything, especially advertising.

The first television ad for Ivory Soap made its debut in 1939. By 1948, P&G, schooled by its considerable efforts in brand-owned radio content, launched its first sponsored television program, *Fashions on Parade,* brought to viewers by Ivory and Prell. A year later the company launched *Fireside Theatre,* which quickly became one of the top ten television shows in America, following *The Milton Berle Show* on Tuesday nights. By the 1950s, according to their own internal records, P&G ran thirteen different shows on television, making it the biggest buyer of TV time and reaching some 90 percent of all households.

As with radio, this new medium was a supple canvas for advertising. According to *The New Yorker*'s Emily Nussbaum, "[TV] was not merely supported by admen; it was run by them." In TV's early years, "advertisements shaped everything about early television programs, including their length and structure, with clear acts to provide logical inlets for ads to appear." By 1970, P&G was spending $200 million a year on advertising, per *Rising Tide*.

Inevitably, different points of view came into conflict. Though the ad men ran TV, there was considerable dissension about the ideal length and structure of TV advertising, and this created a new tension between authenticity and artifice.

What was the most effective TV format for selling products? Was the better model original content that supported brands, like *Mutual of Omaha's Wild Kingdom* or *GE Theater* (hosted by Ronald Reagan and for years one of the highest-rated shows on TV, right after *I Love Lucy*)? Or was it better to interrupt existing programming with a series of, say, thirty-second commercial messages every few moments? If you're born before the year 2000, you know which format won that battle.

One of the key chieftains of this vision was a young man named Pete Rozelle, who in 1959 was appointed the commissioner of the NFL. Rozelle would go on to train the three television networks of the time—ABC, CBS, and NBC—to better capture the drama and pageantry of pro football, elevating it into the unrivaled TV entertainment it is today.

He would also remodel the game to better accommodate ads, creating the incredible money-spinner that the NFL is today.

And so began the golden age of Command & Control, the glory days of American advertising, from the mid-1950s to the early 1990s, when families across the nation gathered around the dinner table or plopped like potatoes on the living room couch to watch TV together. I'm one of those people who actually lived this experience: My family used to eat supper while consuming *Happy Days* or the evening news.

Since options were limited to three networks, an incomprehensible paucity today, we truly were a captive audience, perfect for carpet-bombing with merciless commercials. Many of these ads were repeated over and over again for maximum brainwashing, always interrupting, which sometimes made them . . . annoying.

But for the most part it truly was the golden age of advertising. Artifice and authenticity, albeit briefly, fused. The products were okay and so was the advertising, and the format came to seem unquestionably like part of the media landscape. Content and context enjoyed a certain consanguinity. During this fecund period, the wizards of Madison Avenue, the real-life Don Drapers, would create, in no particular order, a liturgy of consumer characters and calls to action that shaped America and certainly drilled itself into my head:

Mr. Clean; Mrs. Olson; Mr. Whipple; Charlie the Tuna; Aunt Jemima; Tony the Tiger; Betty Crocker; The Quicker Picker-Upper; It's Miller Time; Finger-Lickin' Good; Have It Your Way; The Antidote for Civilization; Mmm, Mmm, Good; We Try Harder; You're in Good Hands; Reach Out and Touch Someone; Plop-Plop, Fizz-Fizz; Breakfast of Champions; the Ultimate Driving Machine; Don't Leave Home Without It; The Real Thing; The Pause that Refreshes; Sometimes You Feel like a Nut; Think Different; Just Do It; Where's the Beef?; Fly the Friendly Skies; A Diamond Is Forever; A Mind Is a Terrible Thing to Waste; When It Absolutely Positively Has to Be There Overnight; Got Milk?; The Uncola; I Want My MTV; Takes a Lickin' and Keeps on Tickin'; Look, Ma, No Cavities; Let Your Fingers Do the Walking; I'd Walk a Mile for a Camel; Give a Hoot, Don't Pollute . . . The list goes on and on.

By the end of this era, advertising had proved itself, according to Michael Schudson's *Advertising, the Uneasy Persuasion,* as "capitalism's way of saying 'I love you' to itself." Other critics were less charmed. In *Fables,* T. J. Jackson Lears blames the rise of Command & Control television advertising for the creation of "a manipulable mass society" and goes on to say, "for many Americans, the corporate ad business was becoming the chief symptom, if not the major cause, of a sick consumer culture."

Then the Internet came along, a tidal wave of toomuchness, and everything—especially advertising—changed forever.

Part Three

The Future of Advertising

Bikes, Blocks, Buildings, Boats—Because Adding Value Is Everything

Let us be a nation of shop keepers as much as we please, but there is no necessity that we should become a nation of advertisers.

—*Punch* magazine, 1848

If I was starting life over again, I am inclined to think that I would go into the advertising business in preference to almost any other.

—Franklin D. Roosevelt, 1942

There is no correlation between people liking commercials and being sold by them.

—David Ogilvy, 1963

Sometime in the fall of 2014, the avatars of Internet advertising commemorated a major anniversary. The occasion was the twentieth birthday of the so-called banner or display ad, the bane of Howard Stern's existence, those discordant digital carnival barkers that continue to torment the bovine civilians who've yet to embrace ad blocking.

As you may have guessed, no one baked a cake. Nobody warbled "Happy Birthday." No one blew out any candles. People may hate them with a passion, but to be fair, most creative thinkers in the media industry were never particularly in love with banner ads, either. For a while, they made a lot of people a great deal of money. But it was hard to imagine anyone celebrating two decades of ugly clutter and frequent exasperation.

And exasperation is truly the appropriate response to banner ads. It's even harder to imagine anyone celebrating a birthday for the banner ad's even less admired younger cousin, the pre-roll ad, the dreaded thing before the thing, the only format in advertising history so neurotically self-aware of its own annoyingness that it provides a countdown to when it can be skipped.

How did it get this way? Where did digital advertising go so wrong? It's one of the industry's saddest ironies. The game-changing communications platforms that came before it, radio and television, had burst out of the gate as fresh canvases on which Adland could innovate, as we saw in the previous section. But the Internet, so seemingly ripe for seismic change, found its earliest advertisers pedaling backward to . . . the folkways of *print*.

Yes, once upon a time, Web advertising was terra incognita. The early players had no idea how to make a buck off it. There was a need for a metaphor that would drive monetization strategies. Since the Internet had "pages," as I noted earlier, it could accommodate adjacent ads.

It worked, at least for a while. Twenty years later, however, many have concluded with great certainty that banner ads are not Web "native," that the Web is most certainly not a magazine. Those banners do not belong there. They never did. A small group of people had decided to jam them in, because they could.

Again: Just because you can do something doesn't always mean you should.

But what, exactly, was the problem?

Of the many dramatic changes that the Web has wrought, the most deleterious to advertising has been the unprecedented economy of abundance it has unleashed. In connecting the world and giving people access to more information and entertainment than any snake oil salesman could ever have imagined, to more content than anyone could possibly consume, the modern Web literally left no additional space for old-fashioned ads. There was no point in being adjacent amid so much muchness; adjacent might as well be invisible.

The Web also unleashed an unholy maelstrom of noise, and pity the instrument that made a tinny sound.

The ad, which for years had been tolerated for its legitimate if secondary status in the media landscape, was rendered utterly superfluous and totally tone-deaf, a victim of the changing context around it.

This incredible abundance had another unintended consequence. For the first time in its checkered history, advertising's time-honored tension, the battle between authenticity and artifice, was officially rendered moot. It did not matter if banner or pre-roll ads were all about clever artifice or intense sincerity; they were all equally ineffective since they were all more or less ignored. There was simply too much going on elsewhere.

But you know this already. You've intuited it or likely even lived it, and I've made the point several times. What is perhaps less appreciated is how the present problems of twenty years of bad Internet advertising have also started to destabilize the ad models of yore, as in those classic sci-fi films in which someone from the future rewrites the past.

Which brings us to the bane of my existence: advertising on the NFL.

Concussed

Every holiday season my family and I fly west from New York City to visit my wife's parents in the rural exurbs of Sacramento. I've been married a long time, nearly two decades. During that period our extended family has expanded and contracted and expanded again, careers have changed, fortunes have been made and lost, children have come and grown, but one thing never changes: *Every Sunday after Christmas we sit around and watch football like the rest of America.*

There isn't much else to do in Sacramento, and rather than fall into tense, contentious arguments about gun control and climate change, we gather around the boob tube with the in-laws for the soothing ritual of watching large men pummel one another for three hours. If we're lucky and the games turn out to be competitive, that Sunday, which now features the obligatory evening contest, can provide three full games—*nine hours plus* of pure NFL bliss. When it comes to mass entertainment capable of delivering electric thrills and mind-numbing tedium, there's nothing quite like five hundred forty minutes of football.

I once had the good fortune to be part of a group invited to pitch for the NFL business. I've always loved the game—I thought I'd grow up to play pro until I came to understand the basic laws of genetics—and I recall what a thrill it was to get a peek inside the league's glimmering Park Avenue corporate HQ, with its dazzling walls of memorabilia and vast owners' conference room the size of a football field.

We were ushered into a (far smaller) conference room, and several resplendent suit-and-tied league executives sauntered in, including the NFL's CMO at the time, who was, somewhat incomprehensibly, British.

We were about to launch into our spiel when another swaggering senior league executive made things interesting by preemptively asking a question: *"Why,"* he demanded to know, *"are we so damn hot now?"*

The question, which hovered there for a moment like a forty-yard Tom Brady bomb, was doubly brilliant in that (1) it made it clear the NFL didn't really need any help and (2) it set up a pass/fail dynamic that would clearly color anything we suggested thereafter.

Moreover, the question had, as Winston Churchill

used to say, the additional benefit of being true. Despite a year in which the NFL had endured a host of galling domestic abuse cases featuring star players while simultaneously confronting increased evidence that its players were at risk of long-term brain injury, the league was nevertheless enjoying historic ratings and historic revenues. (The ratings drop wouldn't come until the following season.)

It was good to be the NFL. I don't recall how we answered the question, but unsurprisingly, we didn't get the gig.

Yes, it's good to be the NFL. But as I slumped there on the couch beside my in-laws in the waning days of 2015, during the penultimate weekend when the outcome of so many games actually matters, it seemed perhaps that the time had come to ask the most heretical of questions: Is it still good to *watch* the NFL?

Indeed, was the viewer still in line with the times? Nowadays, it has become all too common to question, if not indict, the game's brutality and its often tone-deaf resistance to change. The *Redskins*—really? Was football simply too barbaric to go on? Was that why ratings had dropped after years of growth?

Maybe, but that's not what I'm complaining about.

My beef with the NFL is the advertising, which features its own anachronistic brutality, an approach that seems increasingly out of touch with these ad-blocking times. As I said, I enjoy the brain-deadening pleasure of cozying up for three hours and twelve minutes of ball as much as the next guy, but I couldn't help wondering what my son—the same kid who like most kids now consumed media via channels almost entirely devoid of ads—thought of me while I sat there watching football, not to mention what I thought of myself.

As *The Wall Street Journal* infamously pointed out several years ago in a much-quoted article, the average amount of action seen on the field during a three-hour NFL game turns out to be about *eleven minutes,* with seventeen minutes devoted to replays and seventy-five minutes essentially spent watching the players and refs stand on the field. The rest was advertising, an endless, eyeball-melting sea of it. (I'm using the NFL as a punching bag here, by the way, but this applies to any live sporting event, including of course that most bloated bacchanalia of endless spirit-crushing commercial interruption, the Olympic Games.)

Still, a simple look at the numbers revealed that my question was idiotic: A live football game was still the highest-rated activity on the planet, watched by at least twenty-nine million people, per *The Wall Street Journal,* far outranking anything else on terrestrial television. It was an enigma wrapped in a paradox. With so many people watching, how could they be wrong?

But, again, that wasn't exactly what I was questioning. What I wanted to know was *this:* Did the pleasure of the game, as it had come to be understood, include the ads? Or were the games so compelling that the ads were something viewers were willing to endure? Were the ads, as they were in the increasingly obsolete world of "appointment" TV, the uninvited guest at someone else's tailgate party? Or was the NFL—and by NFL, again I mean all televised sports—the one place left in the media landscape where advertising was still baked into the cake?

These were fun questions to ask. And they were worth asking. Because something really felt different out there. It might not feel different in front of the TV here in Sacramento. But outside, even here in the exurbs, we had Netflix, we had Amazon Prime, we had Uber, we even had remote-controlled drones and intelligent thermostats; disruption was everywhere, changing everything. The future, at long last, had even come to the San Joaquin Valley. The Web, with its bottomless abundance, had rewired our collective minds.

Was it possible that the mass activity of watching football, which was increasingly unlike any other media behavior, had become a massive anomaly, just like the thirty-second ad formats it facilitated? Had football become an outmoded relic that refused to die, like cigarettes, coal mining, and baby seal hunts? Was football just a form of mass hypnosis, providing an overworked nation with a few hours of much-needed solace from the trying demands of actual thinking?

I realize that the vast audience under the NFL's spell makes my point highly suspect. For who could fault any brand manager for trying to reach every eyeball in America by advertising during these games? Marketers rarely if ever get fired for buying airtime on the NFL. Marketers also rarely if ever get fired for advertising on Facebook. In the age of fragmentation, these were the only ways left to reach a massive audience.

But did the message actually touch all those people? That was the real question. Let's come back to my previous point. I submit, yet again, why watching football is often such a drag: the interminable commercials. They say that some things never change, but nothing never changes quite like the commercials that appear during a professional football game. Just as they've done for half a century, just like the inevitable arrival of yet another Brady-Manning championship game, these tedious thirty-second pests appear like a miniature plague of locusts every few minutes to interrupt the "action."

And the commercials on NFL games never really evolve. In a world of such rapid disruption, when individual players can make international news by taking a knee during the national anthem, the banal familiarity of the NFL's commercial structure could almost be called comforting in its obdurate resistance to progress. With the possible exception of a few experiments with user-generated content and the now obligatory inclusion of hashtags and other social media posturing, the commercial spots you see during a football game haven't evolved since 1972. And you see lots of spots: The average allotment on any given Sunday clocks in, as it has for years, at *more than one hundred ads*.

The ads during regular-season NFL games are, as they always were, very much of a piece. During one single afternoon, as I plunged deeper and deeper into catatonia amid the fluffy pillows of a massive couch, I watched cliché-ridden thirty-second spots from the likes of A1 Steak Sauce, Burger King, Chevy, Ford F-150, Microsoft, KFC ("Yep, we're filled up"), Coke ("Make someone happy"), Macy's mattresses sale, Southwest, State Farm, Nissan, Toyota, Verizon, Sprint (vs. Verizon in a cheeky attack ad), as well as myriad promotions for a handful of new Fox shows and Fox's *Ultimate Fighting Championships*. The few players who broke the mold with a semblance of wit—Geico, Android, a clever new campaign from DirecTV called "The Settlers" (*That's what we do,*

son, we settle)—felt like a cherished relative one prayed to
be seated next to at an endless family reunion.

What almost all these spots had in common was that
they were uniformly bad, almost parodies of what one
expects to see, seemingly designed by committee or spat
out by robots, devoid of ideas, almost perversely conceived to be annoying. A recovering insider like me can
see the strategy showing and the desperate attempt to be
sticky. A civilian might just think of them as an excuse to
use the bathroom. When Bud Light tried a little harder
and did a clever promotion with Amy Schumer and Seth
Rogen, it was more than a breath of fresh air. It was an
oxygen tent for the asphyxiated.

But did these ads even work? Did a clever Bud Light
spot make anyone buy more beer? They must work,
right, or why would so many companies spend so much
money here? Someone, somewhere, had the data to
show that sales went up when the media money was
spent. Which meant that for a commercial to "work," a
brand was required to commit to a ruthless repetitiveness
that meant bombarding us with a message so many times
that the brain damage made it impossible to forget. Many
of the same spots ran over and over during the same
game—this one *again,* really?—evidence of the assumption that a single exposure would be less effective than
multiple flights. But how many Toyotathons could one
celebrate before such festivities lost their charm?

It must also be noted that almost all the commercials one sees on any given Sunday are for commoditized, mostly unloved companies that make, with few exceptions, products of limited distinction, themselves all highly ripe for disruption, many of which can only halt inexorably dwindling market share by increasing their ad spends, and whose corporate strategy has formally pivoted from recruitment to retention.

For instance, I recently spent some time with the CMO of a major American company, one that is not particularly cherished, who told me he had no choice but to advertise with the NFL. "It's the only way to reach the masses. And it works," he said, albeit sheepishly. We were in the realm of the lowest common denominator, and there wasn't any denying it. He paused for a moment as his luxury car idled at a red light. "But you know what they say about the masses."

I also spent time with another CMO of a Fortune 500 company who blithely accepted all of the above and was nevertheless committed to innovating his way out of the problem. His company, which was one of the world's biggest advertisers, was officially moving away from "interruption." They were going to try to find a way to add value to people's lives rather than annoy them. Easier said than done, but extremely laudable.

Perhaps the only outlier advertiser during the NFL game I watched that Sunday was Hulu, the television streaming service, the purpose of whose third-quarter spot was *to advertise an ad-free alternative*. Think about it: Hulu was running ads about a product without ads in the middle of the most ad-entrenched mediascape on the planet. Talk about excellent targeting!

And then, of course, there was the Super Bowl. At the start of 2016, *The Wall Street Journal* could publish yet another breathless article indicating that the Super Bowl, the most-watched program in America, was still the best way for advertisers to reach the most people in America, thus justifying an expenditure of an incredible $5 million for thirty seconds of airtime.

The evidence presented, among other quotes from those who had drunk the Kool-Aid, was that Web traffic for the Kia Sorento was 31 percent above average after the game, and that sales surged 13 percent for 2015. I watched that game and don't recall the Kia spot, but perhaps I was in the bathroom. Even the *Journal* acknowledged that "the Super Bowl isn't a panacea," citing a Bud Light Pac-Man commercial that, astoundingly, "didn't boost the perennial Super Bowl advertiser out of a sales funk."

One had to wonder how much longer this ad-besotted holiday could last. Was there a more imaginative way to spend $5 million in thirty seconds? Was there a more effective way? Was there anything that might truly add something to people's lives, any solution in tune with the shifting ways in which we consume media? Maybe. But in the meantime, despite all the negatives, despite all the danger associated with the game, there was little to zero evidence that the NFL's unchanging ad model would ever go away.

Except that advertising was changing everywhere else.

A few days before the fiftieth Super Bowl, I was invited by a media reporter at *The New York Times* for an exclusive sneak preview of some twenty new Super Bowl spots in ten minutes, and to opine extemporaneously. (My opinion, reduced to one sentence—"same old, same old"—would appear as the lead quote in the *Times*'s postgame advertising analysis.)

The new Super Bowl spots ran the gamut, as they always do, from brilliant to hapless. Many were truly great, or as great as anything that had to provide thirty seconds of entertainment on a single calendar day.

But thirty minutes later, I couldn't remember a single one of them. I did, however, remember that I'd just seen more than $100 million of ad spending more or less squandered on a formula that seemed increasingly bankrupt, a formula that really hadn't evolved for half a century in which nearly everything else had. And let's not forget: Those were the ads that would appear during the Super Bowl, when the ad makers were meant to be at their best!

If the advertising screened during the regular NFL season represents the essence of inertia, a fossil trapped in amber, immune to the massive secular change happening everywhere else in the media industry, is there anything out there that represents the future of advertising? Does anyone have any real imagination? Is there anything out there that points toward a more inspiring role for advertisers?

Well, there's always Facebook. As noted before, no one ever got fired for buying ads on Facebook, which was why the company had recently posted a quarterly profit of more than $1 billion, the bulk of which came from advertising.

Another far more welcome answer was just a kiosk away.

Chains, Trains, and Massive Gains

I don't know about you, but I take the train to work. My preferred form of transportation is biking, which I do whenever possible, but weather, dress codes, murderous cabbies, and other issues often conspire against pedaling like a madman through a big city.

I am aware that biking is a distinctly urban form of commuting and that most people drive to the office—if

I'm lucky, you're driving and listening to this right now in an audio format—so the tale that follows may seem irrelevant to some. But I think the larger significance of this story applies to everyone who's ever been exposed to below-average advertising.

Not long ago I hopped aboard a crowded train heading from Brooklyn to Manhattan, as I often do, only to find it quickly stuck between stations. The air-conditioning was malfunctioning, the car was packed, and so we lingered, lodged somewhere between the East River and nowhere, seemingly delayed indefinitely. The audio system was inaudible, not that there was any helpful information forthcoming anyway. Nor had this section of the line been wired for Wi-Fi or cellular service.

It was hard to believe we were more than a decade into the twenty-first century. It's also worth noting that my experience had been prefaced, as is often the case with the New York City subway system, by a too-long wait for the train to arrive in the first place. I'd spent that time contemplating the crumbling paint, frayed cables, oozing stalactites hanging from the ceiling, and other highlights of our increasingly decrepit infrastructure. I'd also watched a rat the size of a Prius amble fearlessly across the filthy tracks.

Anyway, back on the train, stuck between stations, I was too irritated to read. So I looked up, above the enraged or passively resigned faces of my fellow riders, to check out, as I often do, the ads ringing the train's periphery.

Advertising on trains is an interesting channel. Until recently, absent any underground connectivity, this was still one of the few places where people could *not* tune out advertising. As they say in the media business, subway commuters were still "receptive" to commercial messages, where ads felt "native," much in the way they did during the Command & Control days of television. Straphangers were the new couch potatoes.

In the past, most of the advertisers who took advantage of this captive New York audience hailed from the lower end of the socioeconomic spectrum, a willy-nilly series of random pockmarked messages, the most notorious being a creepy poster featuring the waxy pallor of the infamous Dr. Jonathan Zizmor, plastic surgeon of the people. I still wonder about the sort of patient who saw a doctor based on a subway ad.

Recently, however, emerging brands with more sophisticated media strategies were engaging in their own subway dominations, taking over entire lines with their better-than-average ad campaigns, turning the F train into a bright and playful canvas. These were the direct descendants of the early rail posters that the journalist Samuel Hopkins Adams had cited in 1909, though it didn't feel as if the ad revenue was trickling down to commuters.

Nevertheless, it became increasingly common to see a subway car saturated with a campaign from the likes of such admired new companies as Casper, Harry's, Glossier, Blue Apron, or other so-called unicorns; some brands went so far as to wrap the entire inside and outside of the subway car with a single message. Many of these brands smartly eschewed all forms of advertising except subway and podcasts, two places where ads couldn't be blocked and still made some kind of sense. The back of taxis was another place where ads enjoyed a captive audience, especially when the "off" button didn't work.

Anyway, I was looking up, checking out the latest painter on this creaky easel, which is how I made my acquaintance with the colorful new campaign that the good people of Jägermeister decided to place in the subway.

The ads were a basic print treatment. Though the mix of orange, celadon, and forest brown was certainly inoffensive, maybe even pretty, the ads themselves were not especially distinguished from a graphic standpoint.

But it was the copy, which stated the following, that was expected to be remembered:

Be the Night Meister

Okay, sure, I thought. *I'll get right on that.*
As I may have failed to share earlier, I'm a lover of

many alcoholic beverages, some more than others, though, to be honest, I never really understood the appeal of Jägermeister. It's probably just me, or the fact that I never belonged to a fraternity. But ... "Be the Night Meister"? Well, if you say so.

According to *AgencySpy*, Jägermeister spends about $6 million a year on American advertising. And with some of that cash it had decided to remind us to be masterful. Or to master the night. Something like that. Let's give some credit for getting "Meister" in there. One can picture the high fives.

In doing so, Jägermeister had likely allocated a fairly large part of its budget to an idea that, though certainly pleasant, might also be considered somewhat contrived. To be fair, it was a problem endemic to so much product marketing, which required Adland to confect a shtick that consumers might not actually believe.

Staring up at this ad, still trapped between stations, I thought of David Ogilvy's most offensive bromide: *There is no correlation between people liking commercials and being sold by them.*

Dear David, I disagree. It may be one man's opinion, but this ad did not engage or entertain me, and, with all due respect, I'm not sure it touched anyone else. I didn't take a poll of my fellow straphangers, but all one had to do was to look around.

Like so much advertising, its makers had deployed

this communication without considering the context in which it might appear. Now here was Jägermeister's ad in the harsh glare of the real world, adding little in the way of tangible value to the lives of people trapped on an aging train, unable to access their smartphones, forging ahead in a world in which every waking moment was subject to an assault of zeroes and ones on the senses.

The ad was perpetuating a model that no longer made much sense. It added little to nothing to a very complex equation. One could see it in the eyes of the straphangers, none of whom were looking at the ad. They had instantaneously evaluated it as nothing more than noise. Were we supposed to give a hoot?

Of course, it didn't have to be this way.

Big Wheels

Hurricane Sandy slammed into the East Coast on the morning of October 29, 2012, at a particularly bad time: It was high tide, the moon was full, and water levels were already elevated. The storm surge flooded streets and subway tunnels, leaving in its wake, according to *The New York Times,* $75 billion in damages, vast power outages, and more than two hundred dead.

One of the more badly hit areas was the Brooklyn Navy Yard, a waterfront facility along the East River, once home to a teeming naval and shipbuilding operation. Among the casualties that evening were two-thirds of the equipment necessary for the nascent Citi Bike program, which was already months behind schedule owing to software glitches, controversy, and other problems. The storm-inflicted damage inspired considerable schadenfreude. At the time, thanks in part to its role in the financial crisis, Citibank could not have been less popular. The haters rejoiced; even the weather gods were against them.

When Citi Bike finally launched on Memorial Day weekend in May 2013, the following year, one had to be a cockeyed optimist to see even the slightest silver lining. It looked to some as if it was going to be a major flop.

And it most certainly didn't look like the future of advertising.

The mood had been a lot different on August 11, 2011, some two years earlier, when the initial idea for New York's first ever bike-share program was pitched to Mayor Michael Bloomberg at City Hall.

According to former Department of Transportation secretary Janette Sadik-Khan, who helped lead the pitch, Bloomberg wasn't exactly an easy sell. Fortunately, there was already a similar program in London, sponsored by Barclays, which provided key learnings. Most appealing to the mayor was that the NYC bike-share program would be privately operated, at zero cost to taxpayers.

The kiosks, which would number in the hundreds, could be installed in under an hour with a light touch; there would be no digging, unlike in the UK.

The proposed bike kiosks would be solar powered and connect to riders via a smartphone app. The entire system was conceived to benefit the city, down to tourists who might be ambling by; all kiosks would feature local maps. Actual locations would be crowdsourced by real New Yorkers. The city would ultimately receive, per Sadik-Khan, sixty-five thousand suggestions on where to put the bike stands.

The team projected that the bike-share program would generate two hundred new jobs. They projected a $13 million profit for the city, which would come in the form of shared revenue from sponsorship and rider fees, which could be reinvested in other urban initiatives. The mayor, apparently, was convinced.

There was only one problem: City Hall still needed to land a sponsor, one that could pony up an eight-figure investment.

Most brands with that kind of money tend to spend the bulk of it on advertising.

Moreover, Sadik-Khan, who's best known for turning Times Square into a pedestrian oasis, had high standards for any potential partner. "You don't want a grocery store logo up there," she told me. "This was NYC. We needed a brand that matched ours." The city would go on to pitch Nike and Apple, among others, but to no avail.

Edward Skyler is Citibank's EVP of Global Public Affairs. Before his role at Citibank, he served as deputy mayor for operations in the Bloomberg administration, the youngest in NYC's history. It's not uncommon for players to move from public office to the private sector, but Skyler's transition to Citibank in September 2010 created a connection between the two entities that helped make Citi Bike possible.

Sometime in 2011, shortly after Skyler had arrived at Citibank, Sadik-Khan reached out. Skyler made it clear he was certainly willing to crunch numbers and pros and cons, but he would have to be convinced. They both certainly saw the serendipity in the name Citi Bike. After all, it was just two letters away from Citibank. Those bike frames would be a cool mobile canvas for the company's Pantone 286C blue.

Though Citibank was going through a hard time, it had a fairly long and mostly impressive track record of public-private partnerships. Over its two-century history, the bank had financed the Marshall Plan, the Panama Canal, the transatlantic cable, and the space shuttle.

It was clear that a bike program of this size presented risk, but the huge branding opportunity was the clear reward: 2012 was the company's two hundredth anniversary. The entire organization was searching for ways to make a positive statement. Citi Bike offered the opportunity to actually improve how the city operated. In many respects, it was the big swing the company required to match its ambitions and rehabilitate a tarnished brand.

Skyler was enthusiastic, but he knew he would need support from other senior execs. "I didn't think it would be appropriate for me to do what seemed like imposing it or ramming it down people's throats."

The point became moot when his colleagues in marketing got excited, and Citi Bike began to be understood within the company as a very different animal, namely as *advertising*, only in a less familiar form.

This wasn't anything like, say, running a thirty-second television spot during the Olympics. But Citi Bike could, in theory at least, accomplish the same goals as far more traditional advertising: namely, making people feel positive about the brand.

Michelle Peluso is the recently appointed CMO of IBM. Before that, she was Global Chief Marketing Officer at Citibank. Before that, she'd been CEO of Travelocity, the disruptive travel site. She certainly knew how to market a business. And perhaps most important, during her tenure at Citibank, she oversaw the company's advertising budget. She controlled the cash required to make something like this happen.

"Ed called my team and basically said, 'I'm handing this off to you,'" Peluso explained. "'I'm not the marketing person here. I have no idea if this makes any sense.'"

As a marketer, Peluso had been searching for ways "to make Citi real and authentic again." Banks, as noted in the previous section, typically produce some of the less inspired advertising on the planet, often filling the world with communication pollution. Peluso was searching for another way, a search complicated by the fact that her industry was loathed on a massive scale. She knew this wasn't the time to join the clown caravan of NFL commercials. She was also strongly against a proposed idea to bring a full-blown Grand Prix race to New York. That just didn't feel right.

"I felt like we needed to be doing something really good for real people," she told me. "So when Citi Bike first came over the wire, it felt like, yeah, *this* is what we're talking about."

Peluso drafted an internal memo to Citibank's head of consumer finance. The subject: bicycles and why Citibank should stand behind them. Budgets were tight that year, but she was prepared to be convincing. "Our stock had gone from ninety dollars to ninety-nine cents. Understandably, people did not want to take risks. There was always talk that people were going to get killed, that it would be on the front page. Some people decided it was lowbrow. After all, we were an aspirational brand and biking is, you know, *not*."

Part of Peluso's strategy was to use Citi Bike to reexamine the qualitative standards of Citibank's current advertising, and how the bank could do better through better communications, for the city and for its own employees.

"It just felt like we were doing a bunch of traditional advertising, but we weren't really changing the game," she said. In an interesting pivot, the company began to simply look at Citi Bike as a new, more innovative version of its existing out-of-home advertising—an alternative, ironically enough, to the passive ads one sees on the subway and other static billboards or via stadium sponsorships.

Financially, taking down much of its out-of-home advertising to pay for Citi Bike made far more sense, as a preexisting budget could simply be diverted from one channel to another. That helped many of the less enthusiastic internal players get comfortable with the notion. "We were just going to do a few less billboards," Skyler said, "but we were also going to add six thousand *roaming* billboards. And we weren't just putting our name on something; we were helping to create the first new transportation network in New York City in a hundred years."

Of course, this was a bank, and no decision, especially the idea of embracing New York's first bike-share, could be made purely on instinct. Fortunately, initial research indicated positive associations with the concept. So from late 2011 to early 2012, the Citibank team began to investigate whether this was truly something that the company was willing to do, and how it might get comfortable doing it.

Vanessa Colella had taken a circuitous route to the role of Citibank's head of North American marketing. A West Coast native, she'd been a teacher for many years before deciding to get a Ph.D. at MIT and joining McKinsey as a consultant. She'd spent years at Yahoo before coming over to Citibank in 2010. When Citi Bike was first proposed, she was commuting from San Francisco to New York, spending a great deal of time in airports and traffic jams. She had a lot of sympathy for new forms of public transportation.

"The first time I remember it being pitched," Colella told me, "there was a lot of healthy skepticism." Questions abounded: What if the bikes didn't work? What about helmets, for instance? Was this really something that would wind up being a positive thing for the city?

Like all good marketers, Colella was driven by a genuine sense of purpose. "We couldn't just put messaging out to solve our problems; we needed to deliver a service to the community that we thought could make a difference. We had to show, not tell."

Citibank also had to find a way to quantitatively measure the massive risk it was about to manage. That meant justifying the return on investment, which at this point had been tagged at a tidy $41 million over five years. As one might imagine, a great deal of cost-benefit analysis took place. "It's hard to get a mental model of what six thousand bikes look like," Colella told me. "Would this really create enough density to be noticed in this city? We needed to know."

Like Zappos stenciling its brand on airport security shoe trays—a brilliant marketing idea, albeit one that actually did nothing for consumers (except perhaps elicit a not-to-be-underestimated chuckle that made the TSA seem a little less horrible)—Citibank began to see the bikes, and the physical kiosks they required, as white space. They'd created a new channel rather than reflexively defaulting to an old channel so bloated with ads that it was effectively invisible.

(Not long ago I was on a business trip and noticed that the familiar Zappos ad, the one I'd admired at the bottom of the plastic airport security tray designed to hold my shoes, had been replaced by a Sabrett hot dog ad. You couldn't find a better example of advertising at its laziest. Where once a connection had been made between shoe seller and shoe with the whimsical impact of a footprint on virgin snow, we now had the arbitrary insertion of another incongruous message. Dirty soles and meat products: not exactly an appealing association.)

Anyway, instead of putting their message in traditional places where people have long been habituated to ignore them—this was before the widespread arrival of ad blocking—Citi became the Jackson Pollock of their industry, painting in a new way that had never before been seen in New York.

"There is a lot of slapping one's logo on things," Skyler said. "People don't necessarily associate you with the product. Here, we *were* the product."

Unfortunately, much of the press didn't see it that way. As launch day approached, the *New York Post* filed daily attacks on Citi Bike, pillorying the program as a death trap. Perhaps most cruelly, it went so far as to suggest that bikes seemed vaguely French. Meanwhile, Dorothy Rabinowitz, *The Wall Street Journal*'s Pulitzer Prize–winning editorial board member, filmed a video op-ed titled "Death by Bicycle," in which she rabidly attacked the "totalitarians running the government of the city," possibly confusing blue bikes with black helicopters. The video became an instant viral hit. After all, it was hard to resist footage of a befuddled journalist getting apoplectic about . . . cycling.

Good news came in the form of Leonardo DiCaprio, pedaling around New York on a Citi Bike with a supermodel. Other celebs followed suit, as did a Citi Bike cover on *The New Yorker*. Unlike most advertising, Citi Bike seemed to have a gift for generating tremendous earned and free media.

"There just aren't many things we do in this crowded field of marketing that people want to talk about," Colella said. Or, as Skyler adds, "Not only did we get brand uplift in New York, we got it globally. Municipalities all over the world studied it."

Years later, Citi Bike has to be considered a massive, historic success and a game changer in terms of reinventing advertising.

No matter how the company chooses to continue communicating across traditional channels—and Citi Bike remains part of a mix that still includes lots of TV ads and subway posters—they can point to the bike program as an epic win. Given my subway experience, it's too bad it couldn't be a larger part of that mix.

The numbers would certainly suggest making a larger investment. Consider this: When the Citi Bike program rolled out in 2013, it concluded the year with a total of 6.3 million trips. By 2015, that number had risen to 10 million, a 59 percent increase. In the same time, the total mileage by riders had gone from 11.2 million miles to 18.5 million, a 65 percent increase, all according to Citibank's public reporting. By 2015, 93,000 riders had bought annual memberships.

And the so-called brand metrics, the very needle Citibank was trying to move, might be the most compelling: From its launch in 2013 to the fall of 2015, favorable impressions of Citibank have risen some 28 points to 72 percent, according to Citibank's internal data. Meanwhile, the number of people who would consider acquiring a Citibank product has gone up 43 points. Perhaps most remarkably, the program has a nearly flawless safety record. "A big concern was that there would be blood on the streets," said Sadik-Khan. "Today, we have forty-four million miles ridden and zero fatalities."

The truth is, sentiment is a difficult thing to measure, and much time is squandered calculating it. The Citi Bike numbers are impressive, but these data points were created mainly to satisfy bean-counting actuaries. They're the same dusty metrics conceived to measure whether or not advertising actually works, a question that has been disputed for years. What we don't have enough of is data that measure how annoyed people are by bad ads.

The answer, as it turns out, is almost always self-evident, something rarely admitted in advertising. You don't need much more than intuition to see that most people would choose a clean Citi Bike over a useless ad. One accomplishes something, the other doesn't.

"It's not hard to believe that it's better to delight than to annoy," Colella said.

So why don't more brands pursue epic ideas like Citi Bike? Why do so many choose the opposite of delighting us? If there's a lesson to be learned from this story, it's that a critical component to reinventing advertising is a company led by people who believe they must stand for something—*from a communication perspective*. This is an important clarification. It's nice to have principles and purpose, but companies must also bring principles to *how* they advertise, and must accept that this idea— especially in the age of ad blocking—is just as important as *what* they advertise.

Sadly, few companies, especially the ones that spend large sums of money on advertising, consider such principles. This must change or there will be consequences. In an era of unprecedented noise, producing pollution in the form of annoying advertising represents the height of an unprincipled approach and, more worrisome, is likely flat-out bad for business. The correlation may be hard to conclusively measure at the moment, but I believe that bad advertising will increasingly have negative repercussions to an offending company's bottom line.

What will it take for other companies to support such an approach? The quick answer is the right people coming together at the right time. And maybe just a little luck.

"I think it might just be that Citi Bike was a once-in-a-lifetime opportunity," Ed Skyler told me, somewhat depressingly.

Let's hope that truly isn't the case. But it will be, unless more brands take risks.

"It could have been ugly," said Sadik-Khan. "But they set a completely different standard and changed the status quo."

All it requires is imagination, conviction, courage, and tremendous tenacity.

Simple.

Signs of the Times

In addition to my ad-blocking son, I have a daughter. She's nine. Until we watched the Olympics together—an unfamiliar adventure in appointment television that required constant apologies for the sadistic number of interruptions—I think it's fair to say that she'd never seen a commercial in her entire young life.

Please don't think my family toils on a commune or lives like farmers somewhere completely off the grid. Far from it. This is just run-of-the-mill media behavior circa 2017. For despite not ever having really seen a commercial, my daughter has consumed a seemingly bottomless array of TV, movies, and music, not to mention a million or so apps. All it took was on-demand cable or a Netflix or iTunes account. Despite her unreceptivity to traditional advertising, she'd developed a healthy loyalty to a handful of brands, including Lucky Charms, Oreos, Häagen-Dazs, and Justin Bieber, which says a lot about the nutritional standards in my home.

My kid was a particularly big fan of two brands that have brilliantly navigated the end of advertising. These brands have successfully blurred authenticity and artifice, repeatedly seeking to be the thing rather than the thing that interrupts the thing. These brands clearly realize, either implicitly or tacitly, that the commercial canvas on which they would traditionally reach a young consumer essentially no longer exists, and they have both found a better way, earning my profound respect.

Both point to a more palatable path for advertisers and audiences. Both prove that more than ever, creativity will be critical if a brand seeks to engage rather than annoy.

And by creativity I don't mean simply making less annoying ads, which are always welcome. The real goals are big ideas that reinvent or fully replace ads.

American Idol

I first came across the American Girl Doll brand when my daughter downloaded a movie on iTunes. The name of the film was *American Girl: McKenna Shoots for the Stars*. The movie, which was shockingly average, was feature-length (133 minutes) and starred a cast of unknowns, and my daughter was obsessed with it; she watched it repeatedly despite my feeble protestations.

I would soon discover—perhaps the last person in America to do so—that this film was part of an entire ecosystem—books, clothes, jewelry, accessories—designed to support the launch of a new doll named, you guessed it, McKenna.

One could buy the new McKenna doll at one of the many, constantly packed American Girl stores, which, as the name implies, are all over America. The NYC flagship was just off Fifth Avenue. Here one could have brunch with McKenna at the store's restaurant, schedule a hair appointment or manicure with one of the store's many doll beauticians, or even see a doll doctor (apparently several American Girl models have had their plastic digits amputated by jealous dogs). There was also an entire wardrobe line devoted to McKenna. And of course half a dozen other dolls, in the event McKenna got lonely.

By the time my daughter and I left the store, I was

down nearly five hundred bucks but up one very happy daughter. They say money can't buy you love, but American Girl helps dads get awfully close.

Walking out, I realized that the American Girl brand had achieved this stranglehold on my daughter's imagination without her ever seeing so much as a single traditional ad for the company. And yet every inch of the store and its attendant content was advertising. Which was smart, because, as noted, my daughter, like most kids, wasn't seeing traditional ads anyway.

All this very savvy company had done was communicate its values via content, a very old model that was new and necessary again. They'd become genuine storytellers, and put themselves at the center of the story.

It was brilliant. But the brilliance of American Girl pales in comparison to the incandescent genius of Lego's adventure in antiadvertising.

Great Danes

The world's biggest toy company was founded in 1932 by a man named Ole Kirk Kristiansen to "develop the builders of tomorrow," a mission statement that Lego still embraces today. The word "Lego" is derived from the Danish for "play well." It also has the good fortune to mean "put together" in Latin. The Danes pronounce the *e* so it rhymes with "tree"; the rest of us say "lay-go."

Either way, it's a moot point. Lego requires no translation. The product transcends language, as reflected by the company's massive international, generation-straddling appeal. I can still see myself as a child, lost in play, adrift on a sea of multicolored locking bricks; today, my own children continue that tradition. And it's not just kids: Grown-up devotees often attend so-called BrickCons, massive conventions that gather AFOLs—aka "adult fans of Lego." Weird, but true.

The company's small interlocking pieces were originally made of wood, but Lego began making plastic bricks in 1947, long before *The Graduate* made plastics famous. Lego has been a successful concern for years; it's hardly a sleepy foreign outfit. Like Disney and American Girl Dolls, it has diversified its portfolio and extended its brand through original TV cartoons and clever licensing deals with movie franchises such as *Star Wars, Harry Potter,* and *Lord of the Rings*. It opened Legoland amusement parks in America, Europe, and Malaysia, with more to follow.

But something special happened in 2014 that truly elevated Lego to the ranks of the world's most sophisticated marketers: The company found a way to transcend advertising.

"We were not necessarily looking to get into the movie business," explained Jill Wilfert, Lego's vice president of global licensing and entertainment, at a recent conference. Though wildly successful, Lego was known to be a fairly conservative organization. "A movie was too risky," Wilfert said.

Apparently, many players had approached Lego over the years with the idea of a movie, but none had brought an actual story. Although toys, like superheroes, have for years been the impetus behind motion pictures, it was Hasbro's success with *Transformers* that inspired the Hollywood producer Dan Lin to pitch Lego an idea from the team that made the animated hit *Hotel Transylvania*.

Lin was clearly a savvy enough customer to know that this was all about the Lego brand and subverting traditional advertising. "If we tell a great story, it can have a halo effect," he told *The Hollywood Reporter,* effectively implying that a first-rate film could also move the merch.

So Lego swung for the fences and wound up with the world's best ad.

One might expect cynicism for besmirching the prestige of the cinema with such a commercial agenda. Instead, there was almost universal praise.

Take *The Guardian,* for instance, whose spot-on headline was THE LEGO MOVIE ISN'T A GREAT FILM, IT'S A BRILLIANT COMMERCIAL. Or *The American Spectator,* which noted that *The Lego Movie* was "a powerful commercial for a product that links generations."

Everyone seemed to get what was going on here, and, interestingly, they all applauded. A writer at the Australian site *News.com.au* cheerfully asked, "Did I just pay $20 to watch a two-hour ad?" The tech-focused blog *Pando,* whose motto is "Speaking truth to the new power," echoed the sentiment: "Last night I paid $14 to see a 100-minute long commercial in 3-D."

Pando was especially astute about the implications. Its headline was NATIVE ADVERTISING ON THE GRANDEST SCALE EVER ATTEMPTED. I cite this extended quote from the article because I couldn't have said it any better, and because it came from someone outside the ad business. As *Pando's* James Robinson notes:

> The rub is, it's actually a fun film. I'm nearly 30 and it played off my own nostalgia for Lego, making good use of Lego's dizzying array of product licenses to rope in characters like Batman, Superman, Shaquille O'Neal, and Abraham Lincoln into a silly, yet sharply written cultural pastiche. The creators of *The Lego Movie* worked with Lego to tell a story about its brand in the same way as every publication from the *New York Times* to *BuzzFeed* is working with their advertisers. The result was executed on a much larger scale and stage and was something that people wanted to see and pay for. The key is openness. No one

> was tricked or misled. There was no
> mystery this morning why I felt favor-
> ably toward the Lego Corporation.

Exactly. The perfect blend of authenticity and artifice. But then *Pando* blows it. The article's final point is "for better or worse, [*The Lego Movie*] proves we can drink content from the corporate fountain and enjoy it."

Why "for better or worse," dude? Isn't your point that *The Lego Movie* is genuinely good? It is *better,* not worse. Better is . . . better. And by better, let's be clear: I mean it's a lot better than a commercial. Because commercials, even at their best, are something people rarely want to see, and never something people are willing to pay to see. Moreover, we were living in a world where, except for sports, one rarely even saw old-school commercials anyway!

What would be *worse,* much, much worse, is if other brands failed to take notice and continued to fill their corporate fountains with nothing but traditional advertising. What no one wanted was more of those unimaginative old ads slowing down NFL games or blighting the Internet with stalkerlike banner ads.

This is why *The Lego Movie* is so significant. A *brand* made a brilliant, well-executed movie. The movie was a hit. The movie also happened to be an ad, one that people were willing to pay to see.

For the first time in a long time, the thing that normally sold the thing had become the thing itself. There was no adjacency, nothing to sidle up next to. Just a good movie, about a brand, brought to you by that brand. It was primary, not secondary.

This is the lesson advertisers must follow to add value in the future. What we need is better content from brands, and not just product placement, which screams of inauthenticity. We need work like Werner Herzog's lovely *Lo and Behold: Reveries of the Connected World,* which was created for the security firm Netscout and debuted at the Sundance Film Festival. Or the recent feature-length documentary about Martin guitars and an ever increasing array of premium content conceived and sometimes executed by brands as a fundamental alternative to advertising.

And this better approach to advertising doesn't always require making a movie. As Citi Bike demonstrated, change can come in the form of infrastructure.

Or a brand can simply do *nothing,* and choose the dignified and much appreciated idea of sponsoring another quality story without commercial interruption.

What increasingly must be taken off the table is traditional advertising. There's just no room left for that anymore.

• • •

But wait, you ask, how do we know *The Lego Movie* actually worked as advertising? Before I answer that, please remember that traditional advertising is perhaps the only multi-billion-dollar business that is understood to be fifty percent ineffective.

Here's how: Beyond the rapturous reviews, *The Lego Movie* ultimately earned back more than $400 million on a $60 million investment, per *The Hollywood Reporter*. Most brand advertising, the sort seen during football games, doesn't generate any direct revenue, let alone profit. At best, it achieves brand lift, which translates to sales. *The Lego Movie* did that, too, without having to buy expensive airtime.

And here's the kicker: In the first half of 2015, shortly after *The Lego Movie* was released, the privately held Lego corporation became the most valuable toy company in the world, overtaking Mattel, with publicly reported sales over $2 billion a year.

"I'm pretty confident we'll be seeing additional Lego movies in the future," Wilfert recently said with a wink.

Outliers and Expats

A few years ago, the writer Jonathan Safran Foer paid me an office visit. Acclaimed novelists don't usually lower themselves to meet with ad execs, but we'd known each other from a previous project, and Foer wanted to tell me about his recent dalliance on "the dark side," and what an unexpected pleasure he'd had as a part-time marketer for corporate America.

Perhaps there was something to this ad guy thing after all?

As it turned out, Foer had had lunch one day at Chipotle and, like many people, found himself stuck with nothing to read. While looking around, he had a profound if somewhat obvious epiphany: The restaurant was overflowing with what we ad guys call "white space"—myriad untouched surfaces on which one could put media. And he had an idea.

As I mentioned earlier in the Citi Bike story, Zappos once ingeniously put their logo inside the plastic trays you use to pass your shoes through security at the airport. They'd found virgin white space that was also contextually connected to their business, and decided that this was the ideal place to put their brand name. Zappos certainly unearthed an inspired new channel, which isn't nothing, but the average Joe really didn't get anything in return. Perhaps Zappos could also have provided a grant to the TSA or one of our crumbling airports to improve the entire security experience, which is of course soul crushing.

Foer, on the other hand, genuinely wanted to improve the not uncommon experience of eating alone, and to delight the soul. His idea was simple—use Chipotle's burrito wrappers, its brown paper bags, and the sides of its soda cups as canvases for thought-provoking ideas by great writers. The plan could be easily implemented, and he could curate the writers himself. "It's not going to change the world," he'd later say, "but it's better than a blank bag."

So Foer called Chipotle CEO Steve Ells, who was a fan of one of his books. Ells has long championed non-traditional marketing, including a lovely award-winning animated film the company made not long ago called *Back to the Farm*, which is one of my all-time favorite works by a brand. (It must be noted that this lovely film was overshadowed by Chipotle's recent food safety woes, which proves that an unimpeachable product is the ultimate form of advertising.)

Foer's pitch was simple: "Why don't you just *give* something to people? Not as a marketing tool. Just as something thoughtful." When Foer told me this story, I applauded. Then I pointed out an essential paradox: His idea proves that marketing—for what else was this initiative, at the end of the day?—can in itself be something thoughtful.

Thus was born one of my favorite examples of how advertising can make the world a better place, the "Cultivating Thought" author series, which now features engaging work by such luminaries as Toni Morrison, Jonathan Franzen, Malcolm Gladwell, Judd Apatow, Aziz Ansari, Sarah Silverman, and, of course, Foer, all beautifully illustrated on the once empty sides of Chipotle soda cups, wrappers, and brown paper bags. Foer describes the work as "little gifts, a simple way for people to feel engaged."

Cultivating Thought begins with a simple premise: "Must a cup, or bag, suffer an existence that is limited to just one humble purpose, defined merely by its simple function?" It's a good question. And one could pose the same question to the traditional advertising industry. Does function have to define form? And when people increasingly *hate* the form, and actively seek out ways to avoid it, shouldn't we question whether it still functions, and deploy some imagination to rethink it?

Or, as Foer says in Chipotle's video for the program: "It's better to have your mind provoked than not provoked. *Everybody* agrees with this."

Well, almost everybody.

Bitter Pills

"Dad, what's a four-hour erection?"

It's family time again. We're sitting in front of the television, this time in Brooklyn, watching another sporting event, another real-time drama in which it is structurally impossible to avoid commercials, still too much of a hassle to cut the cord.

Some of us are engaged; others are focused elsewhere. The commercials arrive, as they always do during live

TV, every few moments, flighted like a wine tasting, inconsequential and mostly ignored or scanned from a semicatatonic state.

Most of the spots are so anodyne we passively indulge them. Others, like a terrifying new trailer for a zombie apocalypse movie, require the placing of hands over a child's eyes. Then comes the ad for the latest and greatest erectile dysfunction medicine, and a parent caught unawares has some explaining to do.

In his charming but woefully dated 1963 book *Confessions of an Advertising Man,* Madison Avenue legend David Ogilvy opens his final chapter with the following question: "Should advertising be abolished?" When you're forced to confront the side effects of the side effect copy from a Viagra commercial in front of your relentlessly curious nine-year-old daughter, abolition seems like letting the offenders off easy. Having to explain the medical condition known as priapism to a third-grader isn't my idea of fun. Censure or substantial reparations might be a more appropriate remedy.

How little things change. And how much they're finally about to change.

Let's go back to 1963 for a moment. From his then unassailable cashmere tower atop Madison Avenue, Ogilvy surely had the best intentions. The business had made him wildly rich, but his qualms reflected a genuine concern. If his colleagues in the advertising industry would only renounce their "flatulent puffery" and stop foisting an inferior product on a defenseless America in favor of "a more fact-based approach," they would find themselves on the side of the angels.

Remember, back then, just as they are today—and as they've been for a century—ads were regularly under attack. But Mr. Ogilvy was clearly feeling distinct pressure. Apparently, *The New Statesman* had referred to the trade as "vulgar, strident and offensive," and Ogilvy, Adland's genteel chairman of the Joint Chiefs, refused to be part of a villainous class.

Ahead of his time as always, Ogilvy offered a solution that turned out to be astonishingly prescient: "As a private person," he wrote, "I would gladly *pay for the privilege of watching without commercial interruptions.*" It's rare when someone is both the problem and the solution. After all, this is the same man (confirming the industry's eternal conflict between artifice and authenticity) who said: "You must write your advertisements to catch damned fools—not college professors."

But let's go back to Ogilvy's astonishing confession. It's really quite remarkable: Fifty years ago, the man responsible for more advertising than just about anyone else on the planet confessed that *he'd be willing to pay to avoid his own product,* which is sort of like a NASCAR champ publicly clamoring for a self-driving car.

Of course, at the time, it wasn't such a big deal, because ad blocking simply wasn't technically possible. So it was an easy if provocative thing to say, but more or less impossible to do. Commercial interruption was built into the system, a feature, not a bug.

That, as they say, was then. There's no way of knowing if Reed Hastings, the game-changing CEO of Netflix, ever heard Ogilvy's confession, but today's mass adoption of subscription-on-demand services like Netflix and its myriad competitors proves that people will pay to avoid commercials. As Ogilvy had promised, it is a *privilege* not to be annoyed. And you get what you pay for.

Life is just better without commercials. And now it's all just a download and/or a few dollars away. I bet Ogilvy would have used ad blockers.

It won't be long before this is just the way it is. The commercial will be on the outside looking in. "And so we beat on," as F. Scott Fitzgerald wrote at the end of *The Great Gatsby,* "boats against the current, borne back ceaselessly into the past."

Of course, besides the NFL audience, there will inevitably be a few people left who may never pay, and will therefore be stuck watching—and thus perpetuating—commercials. Like the people who still have fax machines and flip phones, they will eventually age out.

Not to get elitist about it, but is that the demo you advertisers actually want, anyway?

• • •

So here I was trying to avoid explaining the medical protocol for a four-hour erection to a little girl. Where have you gone, Mr. Ogilvy?

While we're on the subject of aging men, let's talk about Viagra, not its egregious side effects, but its entire category. It's easy to single out multiple brands for polluting the world with bad advertising, but there may be no industry that collectively squanders more money than Big Pharma.

According to Kantar Media, the pharmaceutical business spent $4.5 billion in 2014 on consumer advertising, with Pfizer, Viagra's parent company, leading the way.

As with Citibank, I don't mean to be unkind to Pfizer. I have friends who are employed there, and I'd like to work with them in the future. The irony is that much of what Pfizer advertises, from critical vaccine research to alleviating pain, improves our lives in demonstrable ways. Much of what Pfizer does is heroic and genuinely in the interest of advancing humanity.

Unfortunately, however, as we saw via the snake oil era, the manufacturers of medicine have long embraced the Machiavellian practice of speaking directly to consumers as a way to influence doctors. This is called "direct-to-consumer," or DTC, advertising, and all pharmaceutical brands do it. These ads, by the way, are required to reveal potential side effects, which tends to make them unpleasant to hear.

In November 2016, "responding to the billions of advertising dollars being spent to promote prescription products," the American Medical Association—the same group that was created to protect the reputation of doctors in an age when doctors were far less trusted—called for a complete ban on DTC ads for drugs (just as they called for a ban on Heroin in 1913).

They had had enough and wanted DTC ads, à la Ogilvy, abolished. The AMA chair-elect cited the considerable negative impact of these commercials and added: "Direct-to-consumer advertising also inflates demand for new and more expensive drugs, even when these drugs may not be appropriate." Again, artifice was at war with authenticity.

Writing about the proposed ban, *The New York Times* sketched out the lay of the land: "Watching television these days means sitting through ads for drugs to ease pain, induce sleep, overcome sexual dysfunction, alleviate depression, ease urinary tract symptoms and more. Some patients say the ads are helpful, but many doctors warn that they are often misleading." This might be true of many DTC magazine ads as well, but TV was where the battle raged most fiercely. Something had to change.

Hence the proposed ban. And now doctors were demanding it!

Did it work? Has DTC advertising experienced an extinction event? In a word, no. Not even close. Nor had a single broadcaster or publisher stopped taking pharma ads. Meanwhile, it's worth noting that there are only two nations in the world that still allow DTC drug ads: the United States and . . . New Zealand.

This, too, will not last. The industry may never embrace the ban, and the beneficiaries of all that ad revenue surely won't stop it. No, it will be consumers who finally make it so, downloading more and more sophisticated ad blockers—imagine one that prophylactically stops Viagra ads—or running to the safety of ad-free platforms where the content they came to see or read or listen to won't be interrupted by a product that in some instances produces headaches, back pain, and, in very rare cases, a four-hour erection.

In upbraiding his industry fifty years ago, our beloved ad guru David Ogilvy encouraged a more fact-based approach as an alternative to ad "flatulence." DTC pharma ads were certainly not lacking in facts, so maybe that wasn't the solution. Ogilvy, of course, just wanted to hear product attributes—cleans faster, cures bad breath, improves battery life—but that didn't really work here, given all the potential side effects that had to be mentioned.

It's fun to think about what pharmaceutical advertising could be doing instead of making commercials about people throwing a football through a tire (get it?) and rattling off side effects in easily parodied laundry lists. Imagine if Big Pharma could once and for all abandon its addiction to artifice and think about communicating authentically.

Here's a thought I alluded to in the first part of the book. I want to repeat it again because perhaps you'll realize I'm serious now. In addition to Viagra, Pfizer also makes medication for depression, a distressing affliction that affects one in ten Americans. It would be churlish and wrong to suggest that this very real condition is caused by repeated exposure to bad advertising. That's clearly not true. But it's certainly behind a great deal of depression.

What could Pfizer do, especially in an age when DTC may one day be banned? What could they produce that aspires to the beauty, utility, ambition, and effectiveness of Citi Bike? What if they used their brilliant minds to truly think creatively and reinvent the communication landscape?

Perhaps they could tell more, and more thoughtful, stories, and tell them wide and far. Maybe they could help produce a probing documentary to raise awareness about opiate addiction in America or a series that documented their considerable research into Alzheimer cures. Or they could divert all that money they spend on DTC ad pollution and contribute it instead to cancer research and simply let consumers know about the decision. Or maybe, as I suggested earlier, they could fix the potholes that pockmark our aging infrastructure, as a patron of the transportation arts.

Our roads and bridges are falling apart. Forget soda cups and brown paper bags—America's interstates, airports, and railroad stations are the new white space. We don't need the thousands of tiny, inconsequential ads that currently blight our transit hubs, we need a big-thinking brand to literally repave the road.

And the American road was certainly where forward-thinking companies were already mobilizing for future battles for ad placement. Case in point: Toward the end of the summer of 2016, another pattern in media started to present itself. Uber, the wildly aggressive and ever expanding ride-sharing company, announced a self-driving-car pilot program in the city of Pittsburgh. At the same time, a new media company called LinkNYC started quietly putting up free super-high-speed Wi-Fi kiosks around the city of New York, where old-fashioned pay phones used to be.

The implication was that our cities would soon be

wired 24/7 and that self-driving cars powered by artificial intelligence would be able to sync to that grid. In other words, sometime between five minutes and fifty years from now, taxi drivers and the trucking industry will be superfluous, displacing an entire workforce and likely making it illegal for civilians like you to drive.

So what will you be doing in the future to pass the time in your new self-driving car? Consuming news, entertainment, or advertising from your windshield, obviously. But what brand would get there first? And would they repeat the same mistakes made by early Internet advertisers and choose annoyance and interruption rather than surprise and delight?

Let's hope not.

Or perhaps Pfizer could provide a few extra ferries.

In the summer of 2016, *The New York Times* confirmed a rumor that had nagged Big Apple commuters for months: The L train, the primary artery in and out of Williamsburg, Brooklyn, which made it the single most hipsterific subway in New York City, would be shutting down in January 2019 *for eighteen months*. The *Times* called it "among the largest disruptions in transit system history."

The shutdown was required for desperately needed repairs as a result of Hurricane Sandy, the same storm whose wrath had set Citi Bike back a year. Thanks to Citi Bike, which had kiosks in Williamsburg as well as Wall Street, some could pedal to work, and think warm thoughts about Citibank while doing so. But that was far from enough. And bikes really didn't cut it in inclement weather.

Was there any lemonade to squeeze from this massive lemon? Didn't anyone, or any *brand,* see this as a huge opportunity? It's fair to say that for most people living in a place like Williamsburg—a demographic, need I mention, that's almost exclusively millennial and thus highly desirable as well as extremely elusive to most advertisers—the concept of "disruption" was generally something to be embraced. Pound for pound, it would be hard to find an area more suffused with disruptive thinkers. But a year and a half without train service, potentially upending some four hundred thousand passengers a week according to *The Wall Street Journal,* was obviously not the kind of disruption all those psychographically attractive young people had in mind.

And it would get worse for the local hipsters. Another headline heralded a coming crisis for the Brooklyn-Queens Expressway, perhaps the most chronically sucky major highway in the country, or as the natives called it, the Brooklyn-Queens Distressway. "BQE Cantilever Work Promises Pain," blared *The Wall Street Journal.* Apparently an entire section of the expressway was literally crumbling, and extensive repairs would be required, ideally before it collapsed. "It's a horrible crappy road," said the NYC transportation commissioner in a moment of rare municipal transparency. "I wish we'd never inherited it."

Nearly a decade of work would be required, at a reported budget of $1.7 billion, inconveniencing some 140,000 vehicles a day. The traffic implications were staggering. It should be mentioned that the BQE is the path one generally takes to New York's LaGuardia Airport, a venue whose disgraceful squalor former vice president Joe Biden had equated with a third-world country—a situation that would hopefully change following a $4 billion renovation, due to be completed in 2019. Where all this repair money was coming from was not entirely clear, given existing budget shortfalls, nor was it clear why the situation had been allowed to deteriorate so woefully in the first place.

Let's recap.

Our planes, trains, and highways are a horror show. What would it take, to borrow a phrase, to make America great again?

The answer, of course, is to reinvent advertising.

As noted earlier, the global advertising industry spends some $600-plus billion a year, with the U.S. market responsible for about a third of that figure. Advertising's own practitioners notoriously admit half of that spending doesn't work, they just don't know which half.

Meanwhile, consumers and context are taking away the canvas for most traditional advertising, making it difficult for many marketers even to know where to spend their money.

At the same time, millions of citizens receptive to commercial messages take myriad forms of public transportation every day. The user experience is bad enough. The bad advertising that attends it rarely helps.

The government is mostly broke and individuals are more or less powerless.

And brands . . . Well, brands are sitting on vast advertising budgets—and are still permitted to flush half of that cash down the toilet. It all seems rather unsustainable.

So let's say it again, because it needs to be said again: What if brands looked to infrastructure as the new official canvas for their commercials? Imagine a Pfizer-branded ferry. An entire airline terminal brought to you by Citibank, rather than filled with random spots and dots. A new light rail line with pleasing colors and comfortable seats, rather than our horrific commuter train system. Why not rename the BQE and put it in the capable hands of HPE—Hewlett Packard Enterprise—and let them run it from the Cloud? They make great products and employ brilliant people, but their ads are invisible, and it would surely be a better use of all that intellectual and actual capital.

What could the likes of Coke or Pepsi or any number of recidivistic brands that blow millions on a thirty-second Super Bowl spot do with thirty miles of interstate? As we saw in the case of Citi Bike, the impossible can happen when the right mix of tenacity and talent aligns.

I'm sure you think I'm joking. That this is some vulgar ex–ad man's idea of a gag. It's not. Such an idea would inevitably face considerable bureaucratic hurdles and the ire of all sorts of advocacy groups. They should get over it. Because the status quo isn't any better and is mostly getting worse. Why not applaud advertisers looking to add value to people's lives rather than annoy them? And speaking of advocacy groups, who's advocating for all those tormented by the increasing uselessness of advertising (other than the ad blockers, of course)?

If you can't beat 'em, join 'em.

Some are starting to do this in small but meaningful ways.

Office Politics

In Super Bowl culture, it is customary for the winning quarterback to smile at the camera and proclaim, *"I'm going to Disney World!"*

Now, I realize that victorious gladiators need vacations, though perhaps not to Orlando. But this ritual was never about the QB's postgame plans. It was always a prearranged paid promotion conceived to charm the world's largest audience. No one, to the best of my knowledge, ever investigated if, say, Joe Montana actually packed a suitcase for Florida, but it didn't really matter: It was all part of the big game's epic distillation of advertising's evergreen tension between artifice and authenticity.

At the conclusion of Super Bowl 50, something odd happened. No one spoke much about the commercials after the game. There really wasn't much work worthy of revisiting, despite all that money spent, and the ads faded from memory like morning fog. Instead, the commercial moment that most marketing pundits found worthy of review emerged from the mouth of Peyton Manning, the oldest man ever to win the big game, the hobbling sheriff who had somehow overcome the prodigiously talented young gun before riding off into retirement sunset.

After securing an upset for the ages and having been presented that massive bully pulpit on which to secure his legacy, Manning—whose promiscuous endorsement work for the likes of Nationwide insurance and Papa John's pizza made him the highest-paid spokesperson in the NFL—told the world, in his immediate postgame interview, that he was going to hug his wife and kids and *"drink a lot of Budweiser."* Moreover, like a crazed parrot obsessed with a cracker, Manning repeated the same exact phrase— *"drink a lot of Budweiser"*—when he was again interviewed on national TV.

The Internet went wild with speculation. Was this a paid statement—Manning's live name dropping was calculated to be worth $3.2 million in media—or an innocent fanboy utterance? Budweiser's head of PR tweeted:

> Hi Internet. For the record, Budweiser did not pay Peyton Manning to mention Budweiser tonight. We were surprised and delighted that he did.

Of course it didn't really matter. It was clear that having a celeb on a big stage "spontaneously" yet sincerely plug your product turns out to be a far better way for a brand to *appear* authentic than the artifice of dropping $5 million on thirty seconds of airtime, which suggests how crazy things have gotten. Despite the protestations of Bud, anyone with any sense could intuit that Manning likely had some sort of commercial agenda, and that shilling for profit was his God-given right and the American way.

But who cares? Free media, not advertising, got people talking about the beer, and likely sold a few thousand extra cases via the power of suggestion. In that sense, even if it wasn't intentional, the Manning/Bud Moment is the most subversively effective Super Bowl commercial of the past twenty years, something to rival the brilliance of Citi Bike, if not quite the same contribution to society. Now think about what could have been done if the principals had actually used their imagination.

After all, traditional advertising was dying. But the need to sell would never go away.

A year or so later, there was reason to believe the powers that be at Anheuser-Busch had learned something after all. Not long ago, I visited the company's new headquarters in the North Chelsea neighborhood of New York City, where AB is building a new flagship office that looks more like an Internet start-up than an old-school beer HQ.

It was once common practice for most companies to speak entirely through their advertising, and the people behind AB and its myriad sub-brands have certainly done a great job at this over the decades. But in an age when even a zillion-dollar Super Bowl ad budget doesn't automatically move the needle, and the traditional canvases for advertising are increasingly being erased, Anheuser-Busch had reportedly concluded that "interruption" was no longer the default paradigm, and that it would spend the bulk of its dollars on sampling (letting people taste the actual product) and content (making movies and TV shows that somehow connected a viewer's imagination to the product).

To attract consumers and compete with the craft beer revolution, AB would have to walk the walk. So it converted a tired old office building into a fancy new space with a microbrewery in the basement, arty graffiti on the walls, an open plan with a big connecting staircase and lots of glass in the spirit of a dot-com, and a club on the roof. Most tellingly, it allocated a chunk of its ad dollars to the construction budget.

That was certainly the strategy embraced by Samsung, the Korean electronics giant, who the previous year had opened a glimmering flagship called 837 in New York's Meatpacking District, not far from the new Whitney Museum, from which it was practically indistinguishable.

Samsung, which had long toiled in the shadows of Apple's retail cool, had filled its cavernous new space with immersive virtual reality exhibitions, 360° films, artists-in-residence, Internet-of-things things like Web-enabled refrigerators, and—the pièce de résistance—a long, tubular "Social Galaxy," a mirrored chamber in which one's Instagram photos were automatically uploaded and displayed for all to see and be seen on a giant curvilinear screen.

How could any traditional ads compete with that? Especially when you could so easily ignore or avoid them?

The lesson: Circa 2017, a brand's office was likely a more impactful form of communication than its advertising.

Actually, your office *was* your advertising.

Unless you're Verizon, in which case you used your office as a massive billboard on which to hang advertising.

No Logo

I'm curious to hear if there's an "official" reason other than "because Verizon owns it and it's a branding opportunity and they don't care about screwing up photos of the skyline because they're assholes."

—That Ugly Verizon Building,
a 2013 Reddit thread

Over the course of 2016–17, anyone with a view of Lower Manhattan, including many soon-to-be-inconvenienced citizens of Williamsburg, Brooklyn, could watch a curious renovation project taking shape on the other side of the East River.

The Verizon building, a windowless thirty-two-story former switching center at the base of the Brooklyn Bridge, was being converted into glimmering office space in the clouds. This beast of a structure that had once been ranked the twentieth-ugliest in the world, an edifice described by an architecture critic as "disturbing," was to be remade into a beauty. Where once there had been solid walls, there was now a curtain of expansive glass windows, exposing some million square feet of posh new office space.

But some things never change, especially when they're rooted in the worst impulses of traditional advertising. Unfortunately, the massive Verizon logo at the top of the building, a logo that has besmirched the iconic Lower Manhattan skyline for years, appears to be staying.

Now, I'm aware this might sound like tedious Naomi Klein–style, no-logo undergraduate nonsense, but this really was corporate boorishness at its worst, plopping your name on something without regard to the context, as if that was a fresh idea, or a gesture without repercussions. Moreover, it was the company's old, now out-of-date logo! The graphic design firm Pentagram had created a new, far subtler one in 2015, but Verizon never updated the version at the top of its building. To be fair, that would have likely cost a lot of money and opened additional cans of worms. It's also worth noting that, in a quirk of New York real estate, Verizon reportedly no longer actually owns the building, just the logo space, like a paid billboard. So it's both inauthentic and artificial.

Meanwhile, tourists and commuters alike can stare at that logo from a crowded ferry or antiquated subway train and wonder what might have been.

What it certainly could have been, and what it still very much remains, is a golden opportunity.

One of the pleasures of working in the ad business has been spending lots of time looking at data, much of it inconclusive or inscrutable. One data point I have come to know well is that most people have an intense dislike for their cellular company.

It's hard to imagine the corporate tool who thought he might induce positive feelings about Verizon by putting a massively ugly and annoying logo at the top of a building in the middle of the world's most beautiful skyline.

On the other hand, it's easy to imagine the warmth one might feel toward Verizon if they were to announce the removal of that logo. Or if they decided to double down on that decision by shifting their local budget for ads no one wants to see, or a logo that no one loves, and instead provided eighteen months of free ferry service to the abandoned millennials of Williamsburg.

Now, wouldn't that reinvent advertising and maybe even sell a few more data plans?

Liberté, Égalité, Fraternité

For the past ten years or so, I've spent the start of every summer stuck in the south of France, attending the Cannes Lions International Festival of Creativity.

I know. It doesn't exactly sound like a hardship. But such is the former ad man's lament; always the bridesmaid, never the bride. For Cannes Lions is not the glamorous film festival with which it is frequently confused, but rather Madison Avenue's biggest boondoggle, an annual ritual that finds the entire industry decamping to a tiny Mediterranean resort town to give itself lots of awards.

Since it debuted in 1954, Cannes Lions has been "the global meeting place for people working in branded communications," which is a nice way to avoid having to say "advertising." Instead of actors and actresses, the legendary Croisette is swamped with sweaty execs from global holding companies in cargo shorts and mandals, sucking on cigars and expensing salmanazars of rosé.

And though it isn't the film festival, given the trillion-dollar gas leak that continues to fuel the planet's collective ad business, Cannes actually attracts its fair share of paid celebrities. Over the past two years, I've rubbed elbows in expensive hotel lobbies with the likes of Pharrell Williams, Bono, Al Gore, Chris Martin, Kanye West, Sting, Kim Kardashian, Ryan Seacrest, Anna Wintour, Anderson Cooper, Will Smith, and that master marketer, United Nations secretary general Ban Ki-moon.

Madison Avenue's increasingly contrapposto relationship with the media business means the big ad-supporter players must also make the pilgrimage to Cannes. Here one can find the likes of Time Inc., *The Economist, The Guardian,* Condé Nast, News Corp., *The Daily Mail, The New York Times,* Bloomberg, the *New York Post,* Fox, Viacom, IHeartMedia, and CNN, all hosting fancy parties or private dinners, singing for their supper.

Unicorns and new-media darlings attend as well. Airbnb, Snapchat, Shutterstock, Spotify, Hulu, Vox, and Twitter now all show up, too, as do a host of faceless "ad-tech" companies looking to solve the mysteries of consumer behavior with big data or proprietary algorithms and obnoxiously large rented yachts.

All the media companies are here to flash their wares and increasingly fragmenting audiences to the many global brands in attendance, kicking and scratching to maintain the affections of Pepsi, Coca-Cola, Unilever, Procter & Gamble, and the two dozen or so other big spenders who still fly the ad industry in business class.

And lording over everyone, with imposing oceanfront installations, are what one ad executive called the dons of Duopoly Beach: Facebook and Google, now the beneficiaries of nearly 60 percent of all that annoying Internet advertising, per *Adweek,* to the tune of nearly $60 billion in annual revenue and the chagrin of the increasingly irrelevant incumbents.

The Cannes Lions motto is "We believe passionately in the power of creativity," and who could argue with that sentiment? Indeed, strolling around and attending award shows, one can see the indisputable creative fire-power of Adland, the part I love so much about this business and the quirky people who populate it, and how all that talent is often deployed to unpack issues like the global water crisis or refugee migration. For instance, Ban Ki-moon was there to announce an ad agency collaboration to address hunger, inequality, and climate change.

Though to be honest, most of that talent is still deployed to make TV commercials or banner ads selling sugary drinks or salty snacks, which perhaps isn't the best canvas for creativity anymore.

But thus has it always been. That constant conflict between authenticity and artifice is why the advertising industry has such an unrivaled flair for self-flagellation. Normally, however, that self-deprecation doesn't travel to France. The industry may be constantly debating its own worth, but in Cannes, one could embrace myopia and celebrate ads for the sake of it, free from the anxieties of an uncertain future. After all, money was still being spent and inertia was surprisingly resistant to reality, even if it meant turning a blind eye to the growing disconnect between what Peggy Noonan would call "the leaders and the led."

But the summer of 2016 was different. Something felt strange and unstable. That year, a new blight was casting a pall over the Cannes ceremonies, and much of it had to do with the implications of ad blocking. Could the rise of the blocker, and the consumer outrage and empowerment it implied, mean that the end was finally nigh?

One senior client, Brad Jakeman, president of Pepsi-Co's global beverage group, wasn't ready to say that all advertising was totally dead. Just *bad* advertising. "We're here celebrating 0.5 percent of the work that actually gets made. The other 99.5 percent of the work is generally crap," he said at a panel hosted by *The Wall Street Journal*. He lamented the "digital landfill" the industry was digging.

It was nice, as always, to hear a senior executive speaking truth to power. But all this Howard Stern–style hand-wringing was getting old. Perhaps it was time for the industry to actually start practicing what it increasingly preached, and to embrace change at scale rather than simply celebrate the 0.5 percent of its collective output that wasn't garbage.

It was an interesting thought, and one simply not discussed enough at Cannes or anywhere else the high priests of the profession gathered. What, exactly, would advertising look like if 99.5 percent wasn't crap? Even a 50 percent commitment to higher standards would mean $300 billion channeled away from that fetid landfill. How many people would block something useful? Or something truly entertaining? Was there any going back? What was the path forward? Could the parking lot we'd put up be razed for some sort of paradise? Would anyone ever turn down a free ferry?

Everyone knew change was coming. The only question was when. And what would it look like? On that score, no one was perfectly sure. It just couldn't be annoying.

Let's return to Procter & Gamble, the company that helped invent and innovate so much advertising as we know it. Shortly after Cannes, I rang up Jim Stengel, the former longtime CMO of P&G. For a decade or so, the extremely respected Stengel was arguably the most powerful man in advertising, presiding over an annual marketing budget of more than $10 billion. If there was anyone who could envision the future of advertising based on the failures of the present and past, it was Jim, who today advises brands on how to do better.

We talked about the mood at Cannes, the repercussions of some fifty years of Command & Control, the "live read" and the golden age of radio, the return to "content," and how sponsored TV might be making a comeback. Like most people with any pattern recognition in the business, Jim increasingly shares the sense that the chickens have come home to roost, that advertising, as we knew it, is not long for this world. Deck chairs, *Titanic,* etc.

"You can tell a million miles away if someone's paid to do something," Stengel told me, observing, as so many have, that relevance could no longer be purchased.

He paused for a moment to think. "We're still going to have to make people aware, we're still going to have to sell something." Selling, he said, would no longer be about telling. It would be about standing for something, about communicating a sense of purpose that transcended the pure demands of commerce.

A mere three months later, it seemed the feeling was spreading. In September 2016, many of the same American ad industry mandarins who convene for cocktails in Cannes flew back across the Atlantic to attend dmexco, a big media conference cum boondoggle in Cologne, Germany.

Dmexco promotes itself as "the global and business innovation platform of the digital economy," and lo, here they all were: executives from Google, Facebook, Procter

& Gamble, *The Washington Post,* the ANA (Association of National Advertisers), and the IAB (Internet Advertising Bureau), among others. It seemed like a fortuitous place for the defenders of the faith to make some news.

And sure enough, a bold proclamation soon followed, according to *Adweek.* The announcement was the formation of the Coalition for Better Ads, a new consortium made up of the aforementioned participants. They had all joined forces to "improve the consumer experience with online advertising." At long last, Howard Stern—along with everyone else—had officially been heard.

Unfortunately, the Coalition for Better Ads, which is committed to improving standards and best practices, which was certainly laudable, had failed to lay out a set of guidelines, or any sort of manifesto, that could arm the increasingly embattled advertising industry with a North Star so desperately needed to embrace innovation. Perhaps it was too much to expect a trade organization with a vested economic interest to question advertising's ongoing existence. But there was no "throwdown," no official rules of engagement, no bill of rights. No one at the Coalition for Better Ads was asking if advertising still made sense. Or if ads still had the right to exist. There was seemingly nothing in its charter that people seemed willing to fight for.

So I thought I'd take matters into my own hands

(with some help from a few of the finest thinkers in Ad-land).

Herewith, an official set of checkpoints conceived to subvert business as usual. Because without a higher purpose, without infusing a set of moral principles into advertising's best practices, I fear that the ad-blocking revolution will just continue to expand.

Ten Principles for Better Advertising

1. **Context** is as important as content: In a world of unprecedented abundance, think about the constant sea of clutter your audience swims through on a daily basis. Why would anyone tolerate an uninspired message? Live in fear of institutional myopia. Think about *where* the ad will appear and if it will be welcome.

2. **Manners** matter, even in advertising: Don't be rude, behave yourself, avoid being the uninvited guest at someone else's party, and never bring cheap beer. Deliver the marketing equivalent of a thoughtful housewarming gift. Make advertising that's more altruistic.

3. Just because you *can* doesn't mean you *should:* Consider the possibility that the best thing might be to **do nothing**. Subsidize silence, demonstrate restraint, provide a joyously ad-free experience.

4. NOGAS: Always assume that no one gives a shit. Make them care. Our ability to **tell interesting stories** is what separates us from other species. So say no to your lizard brain and actually be interesting. Create ads that people want to seek out, not screen out. Accept that anything superfluous will be instantly discarded. Be the thing, not just the thing that sells the thing. Try a little harder. Hire more quals if you've got too many quants. More than ever, *creativity is a business imperative.* Recognize that great ideas are rarely produced by committee and almost never flourish under fluorescent light. Moreover, the ad industry is lousy with inbreeding. You can't evolve without mutating the species. Import artists, storytellers, investigative reporters, typographers, couturiers, poets, and particle physicists—anything to shake things up. One of my favorite moments at my former agency was when an intrepid creative director took the entire staff to the Alexander McQueen museum show.

5. If you can't be interesting, be useful. Embrace utility. **Add value.** Do your customer a solid. Provide a service. Support the arts or emerging platforms. Ban the antiquated word "digital" (because what isn't?) and look toward physical

canvases, which are far more welcoming to ads. Use your marketing budget to fix a bridge or repaint a building or gift new instruments to an underfunded high school.

6. Microtargeting people with ads they don't want, no matter how sophisticated the underlying technology, is merely a more elevated form of **junk mail, to be avoided at all costs**. A targeted coupon or a contextually relevant discount is a far superior idea. But only if your customer has opted in. Brand love requires loving the customer back.

7. **Data is a tool, not a product.** As we've seen with fake news, there's a cost to the hegemonic power of clickbait. Use insights to paint more informed pictures, obviously. But also stand up and admit that an artificially inflated audience or a .02 percent open rate in any industry other than advertising would be considered an abject failure.

8. Measure what actually matters: How about calculating the real damage incurred by being annoying? Traditional ROI metrics put us in this predicament, so let's fundamentally redefine ROI. It's time for the industry to toss out our old reporting techniques and invent an entirely new measurement system rooted in hearts and

minds and **humanity**. No one actually pays a price for making bad ads. Imagine if we could precisely calculate the long-term cost of irritating people.

9. **Intuition is one of the great gifts we were given by the gods:** the ability to know in our bones when something is working. Unfortunately, it's a skill that's woefully undervalued in the ad business. If you suspect your ad is bad, imagine what the civilians think. Stand up to the research guy who says that something isn't working, or that something bad is working, when you know with every fiber of your being that he's missing the larger implications. If your company leadership doesn't concur, quit.

10. Vine, the Ringling Brothers circus, Friendster, horseshoes, pay phones, typewriters, etc. **Things go out of business.** Don't think it can't happen to Madison Avenue. Adapt or die.

Advertising will continue to take its lumps. Like everything inherently unwanted, from stale pastries to last season's social media, it was doomed to be overshadowed. Like pollution, we prefer it in the landfill rather than randomly strewn along the road. People, platforms, and products will have to distinguish themselves by doing something radically different, will have to embrace the not-so-radical idea of always endeavoring to be useful, authentic, original, and/or interesting. This will require talent, courage, and conviction.

So who's with me?

Good.

Now, let's connect a few forward-thinking brands to one of those much-needed ferries, hand out free tickets to all our friends, and set a course against the current, heading fearlessly toward the horizon.

Acknowledgments

Given the nature of this book, it's important to note that the immense support I received from the people named below should not be confused with an endorsement of my views.

It would be inconceivable to write a book about Adland without expressing profound gratitude to David Droga, who rolled the dice on me years ago for what turned out to be a very wild ride. David's commitment to quality work is a constant inspiration. His own thoughts on creativity and how the advertising industry can do better will always far exceed mine. I'd also like to give a shout-out to all my other Droga5 colleagues past and present who tolerated and taught me so much, including but not limited to Jonny Bauer, Judd Merkel, Sarah Thompson, Ted Royer, Duncan Marshall, Julia Albu, Mindy Liu, Ji Lee, Mike Densmore, Chet Gulland, Scott Witt, Hashem Bajwa, Susie Nam, Vaughn Allen, Kevin Brady, Neil Heyman, Sally-Ann Dale, Nick Phelps, Colleen Leddy, Bryan Yasko, Becky Wang, Amir Feder, Maura McGreevy, and so many others. I thank Ari Emanuel and Patrick White-sell for seeing the value in their collective vision. And Henry Silverman, Tom Christopoul, and Marty Edelman for confirming it.

And Michael Hainey for the food pellets and fresh water.

Michael Beruit for the generosity and grace.

You can encounter some of the most wonderfully intelligent people you'll ever meet while toiling at the intersection of media and Madison Avenue. Though I have met, worked with, and been tutored by many greats, I've had the privilege of talking shop way too often with the following people, all of whom have in some way shaped my point of view and/or called bullshit on my unfocused ideas. In no particular order: Andrew Rasiej, Nile Rodgers, Antonio Bertone, Simon Dumenco, Jim Cooper, Michael Wolff, Morten Albaek, Tina Brown, Rodney Williams, Meredith Levien, Tina Exharos, Jonah Peretti, Jim Stengel, Eli Pariser, John Meneilly, John del CeCato, Ben Lerer, Wendy Clark, David Kuhn, Soraya Darabi, Philippe Krakowsky, Bob Pittman, Choire Sicha, Richard Edelman, Martin Sorrell, Karen Wong, Matt Harrington, David Remnick, Wenda Millard, Michael Bloom, Derek Hewitt, Dana Andersen, Randall Rothenberg, Joshua David, Eric Hadley, Strauss Zelnick, Janette Sadik-Khan, Edward Menicheschi, Justin Stefano, James Edmund Datri, Lindsay Nelson, Philippe von Borries,

Adam Moss, Brad Jakeman, Mark Thompson, Bill Konigsberg, Jeff Gordinier, Michael Kassan, Becca Parrish, Scott Omelianuk, Sydney Ember, Patrick Milling Smith, David Pakman, Dan Salmon, Ken Kurson, Martin Puris, Jim Friedlich, Noah Kerner, Jim Rutenberg, Ken Lerer, Jim Dolan, Dan Peres, Bob Saffian, David Carey, Dave Etherington, Phil Thomas, Sarah Hofstetter, A. G. Sulzberger, Colin McConnell, Jason Hirschhorn, Andy Weisman, Bryan Weiner, Jolie Hunt, Maryam Banikarim, Jess Cagel, Joseph Meyer, Jim Griffin, Virginia Heffernan, Jesse Angelo, Andrew Solomon, Scott Belsky, Dan Porter, Steven Wolfe Pereira, Jess Cagle, Terry Kawaja, Anita Elberse, Lewis Dvorkin, David Kenny, Paul Caine, Edward Skyler, Jonathan Mildenhall, Shelley Zalis, Bonin Bough, Shane Rahmani, Jonathan Wald, Ivan Bart, Leslie Stevens, David Brinker, Peter Lattman, Michael Hirschorn, Sophie Kelly, George Pyne, Lou Paskalis, MT Carney, Sean Garrett, Hozefa Lokhandwala, Mike Lazerow, Howard Mittman, Laura Brown, Michelle Peluso, John Cantarella, Christian Muirhead, Jeff Benjamin, Jeff Levick, Nick Denton, Gene Pressman, Adam Stotsky, Neil Blumenthal, Eric Ryan, Keith Grossman, Jeff Bercovici, Rupal Parekh, Brooke Hammerling, Scott Dadich, Dan Galpern, Steven Rubenstein, Jeff Raider, Michelle Horowitz, Gary Vaynerchuk, Sean Sachs, Christine Osekoski, Greg Clayman, Noah Robinschon, Joe Marchese, Matt Edelman, Jonah Bloom, Scott Donaton,

Jane Barratt, Bren Byrne, Craig Seligman, Ben Palmer, Andrew Siegal, Doc O'Connor, Teressa Iezzi, Emily Weiss, Rob Norman, Ian Schafer, Gail Heimann, Claire Atkinson, Gil Schwartz, Holly Lang, Jon Steinberg, Bob Sauerberg, Jeffrey Leeds, Pam Wasserstein, Mo Koyfman, Justine Rosenthal, Chip Kidd, Isaac Lee, Bob Safian, Dave Cascino, Billy Paretti, Jay Haines, George Parker, Stuart Elliott, Brian Morrissey, Jonathan Safran Foer, Stephan Paternot, Lawrence Burian, Chris Fralic, Wendi Lazar, Aryeh Bourkoff, Fiona Carter, Jon Fine, Jared Kushner, Erik Moreno, Chris Hughes, Brit Morin, Tony Hendra, Sapna Maheshwari, Alex von Bidder, and Jerry Wind and Catherine Hays at the Wharton Future of Advertising Program. I have surely left someone critical out, and for that, I am deeply sorry.

Matthew Weiner, that show was pretty damn good.

On the publishing side of the aisle, I owe a special debt of gratitude to the indomitable Julie Grau, whose constant support and high standards never fail to inspire; to Chris Jackson for being the all-knowing connective tissue between Sarah Silverman and Jay-Z and everything in betwixt; to my editor, the unflappable and relentlessly upbeat Emi Ikkanda, for her warmth and patience, and for imposing effortless order on what was so often incoherent; and to the entire extended team at Spiegel & Grau and Penguin Random House for their support.

Special thanks to my agent, Andrew Wylie, for his elegance and tenacity.

I am deeply indebted to my colleagues at Tribeca Enterprises, especially the great Jane Rosenthal, whose entire life is a testament to the healing power of storytelling and creativity. And to her Tribeca cofounders, Robert De Niro and Craig Hatkoff, for giving me the privilege of such a thrilling and purpose-driven position. To Paula Weinstein, Ian Daly, Tammie Rosen, and all my fantastic colleagues at the Tribeca Film Festival, Tribeca Studios, and the Tribeca Film Institute, whose good work is a constant source of pride.

To the entire Castaldo clan for their generosity and good cheer.

To Roberta and Bob, for everything.

And one final thank-you to my amazing family—Meg, Sidney, Gemma—for their profound love, support, patience, and understanding. I'm lucky for such good fortune.

A Note on Sources

Just as there are too many ads, there is no shortage of books about the advertising business. To support my particular glass-half-empty take on the pros and cons of Adland, I dutifully tried to read them all. Though I deeply enjoyed (almost) every volume, and read a few of them twice, some books I attempted to absorb turned out to be woefully outdated and thus didn't make the cut.

The scholarship deployed in the tomes cited below was hugely helpful, but nothing truly assisted me in terms of relevance and research quite so much as the steady prose of the men and women who write for *Advertising Age* and *Adweek,* the rock-solid trades that tirelessly chronicle the industry, filling their pages with a constant buffet of news, data, factoids, anecdotes, and opinion. I'd be nowhere without them. Equally invaluable was the ace marketing coverage of *The New York Times* and *The Wall Street Journal.* A dozen other media and marketing sites including *Business Insider, Digiday, Tech Crunch, The Verge, Recode, Campaign, Bloomberg Businessweek, Fortune, Forbes, Harvard Business Review, eMarketer, moreaboutadvertising.com, mckinsey.com,* and *Agency Spy,* among others, kept me constantly looped in and informed. I could hardly crawl, let alone walk, without their work.

On the hardcover front, I took particular pleasure tucking into the tetchy wisdom of the late David Ogilvy, whose *Ogilvy on Advertising* (Vintage, 1983) and *Confessions of an Advertising Man* (Southbank, 1963) are must-reads for anyone interested in the good old days. I was humbled by the rich reporting of *Advertising, the Uneasy Persuasion* by Michael Schudson (Basic Books, 1986); *Fables of Abundance: A Cultural History of Advertising in America* by T. J. Jackson Lears (Basic Books, 1995); *Advertising: The American Dream; Making Way for Modernity* by Roland Marchand (University of California Press, 1985); and *Where the Suckers Moon* by Randall Rothenberg (Knopf, 1994), which is perhaps the best book ever written on a single ad campaign.

Other key works that helped me in ways large and small include *On Brand* by Wally Olins (Thames & Hudson, 2003); *Tono-Bungay* by H. G. Wells (Macmillan, 1909); *For God, Country and Coca-Cola: The Definitive History of the Great American Soft Drink and the Company That Makes It* by Mark Pendergrast (Basic Books, 2013); *Beyond Advertising: Creating Value Through All Customer Touchpoints,* by Yoram Wind and Catharine Hays (Wiley, 2016); *The Great American Fraud* by Samuel Hopkins

Adams (Colliers, 1905); *Game Changers: The Evolution of Advertising,* edited by Cannes Lions with Peter Russell and Senta Slingerland (Taschen, 2013); *Forty Years an Advertising Agent, 1865–1905* by George Presbury Rowell (Forgotten Books, 1906); *Keeping Everlastingly At It Brings Success* by Walter Marden Ringer (Foley, 1977); *Grow: How Ideals Power Growth and Profit at the World's Greatest Companies* by Jim Stengel (Crown, 2011); *D&AD 50* (Taschen, 2013); *Television Is the New Television: The Unexpected Triumph of Old Media in the Digital Age* by Michael Wolff (Portfolio, 2015); *Aspirin: The Remarkable Story of a Wonder Drug* by Diarmuid Jeffreys (Bloomsbury, 2008); *Rising Tide: Lessons from 165 Years of Brand Building at Procter & Gamble* by Davis Dyer (Harvard Business Review Press, 2004); *The American Disease* by David F. Musto (Oxford University Press, 1999); *Heroin Century* by Tom Carnwath and Ian Smith (Routledge, 2002); and the great *Within the Context of No Context* by George W. S. Trow (Atlantic Monthly Press, 1980). The collected works of Mark Twain were a constant inspiration, as were the writing and advisory staff of *Mad Men,* who did so much heavy lifting for me.

A fascinating 1998 article in the London *Sunday Times* by Richard Askwith helped unearth the connection between Aspirin and Heroin, following a conversation with Jim Griffin. In researching the history of both drugs, I found the intrepid work of Professor Walter

Sneader invaluable. Christopher Cohen helped dig through hundreds of documents and offered an incredibly insightful synthesis of way too much information. Stefan Kruecken provided extremely hard-to-locate archival information and translation.

I'm also indebted to the Wolfsonian Museum in Miami, whose unrivaled collection of advertising arcana entertained and informed and made for several transformative days during a tropical storm in southern Florida.

About the Author

ANDREW ESSEX is the CEO of Tribeca Enterprises, parent company of the Tribeca Film Festival. Prior to that, he was the CEO of celebrated advertising agency Droga5. The firm won multiple "Agency of the Year" awards and has been praised in *The New York Times, New York* magazine, and *The Guardian,* which dubbed it "the most exciting agency on the planet." Essex serves on the board of the American Advertising Federation and is the co-author of *Chasing Cool* with former Barneys CEO Gene Pressman and former Noise CEO Noah Kerner, and *Le Freak* with Nile Rodgers.

Twitter: @AndrewEssex

To inquire about booking Andrew Essex for a speaking engagement, please contact the Penguin Random House Speakers Bureau at speakers@penguinrandomhouse.com.

About the Type

This book was set in Bembo, a typeface based on an old-style Roman face that was used for Cardinal Pietro Bembo's tract *De Aetna* in 1495. Bembo was cut by Francesco Griffo (1450–1518) in the early sixteenth century for Italian Renaissance printer and publisher Aldus Manutius (1449–1515). The Lanston Monotype Company of Philadelphia brought the well-proportioned letterforms of Bembo to the United States in the 1930s.